ONCE UPON
A
LIFETIME

Sandra Fletcher

*This story has been written for my children
Jacqueline, Anthony John & Nicola.*

ACKNOWLEDGEMENTS:

I wish to thank DON WESCOTT who gave me the inspiration and confidence to write the original manuscript. To NORMAN FLETCHER for the encouragement that he gave me to continue and a special thanks to SHARON BROOKS and ALISON SMITH who helped me throughout.

PREFACE

Pop Edwards never caught the train home from Northampton that afternoon. Instead, he got a lift home in the back of his mate's pick up truck with Taffy from Cardiff. He hadn't seen Taffy for over four years and you can imagine, the conversation that afternoon was not only about the weather. In fact, it was a good thing no ladies were present.

In the pub later that evening over a pie and a pint, their conversation turned to things that happened during the war.

"We were getting bombed pretty well every night," said Pop. "One particular night there was a crash. We thought 'what's that', because it didn't sound like a normal bomb. It wasn't until the next day we heard that the house at the top of the hill, near to where we lived, had been practically demolished. There was an enormous land mine in the middle of the street. The local children, not realizing what it was, were playing on it, taking home bits as souvenirs. It's a wonder none of them were killed."

Since the beginning of the war, many strange things had happened, but what fascinated Taffy was the story of when a land mine exploded shortly after Christmas 1941 in Llandaff, Cardiff. Apparently, a family returned to their home after spending the night with relatives and found all the tiles of their house had been blown off the roof. The windows had been blown in and the front door was up the stairs. Believe it or not, all the Christmas cards were still on the mantelpiece untouched. All the lampshades had been smashed but the bulbs were still intact, and most remarkable of all was that a tin of fruit, which was opened much later, was found to contain powdered glass. The blast had blown the powdered glass through the wooden doors of the sideboard, through the tin and into the fruit. It was unbelievable.

The landlord of the pub called last orders, and after putting the world to rights, the two friends went home to their respective families and promised to keep in touch after the war.

CHAPTER ONE

The house where we lived was built long before the Second World War and from what I was told, after Mum and Dad got married in nineteen thirty nine, when my Mum was nineteen, the landlord gave them the chance to buy the property, for only nine hundred pounds. The house itself was separated into two flats. Cissie, my Mum and Bert, my Dad, who was seven years older, lived upstairs. Downstairs, another young couple lived with their two young children, Maureen and Keith.

During the war, after a lot of soul searching, Mum and Dad decided to buy the property as it stood. The only difference was that they would now be responsible for all the upkeep of the property. Not only that, but Dad had to arrange for a new rent book to be issued to Mr and Mrs Drayton, the couple who lived downstairs, as he would now be the landlord of number twelve. Charlie and Eileen Drayton didn't like the situation at all.

The house was a typical town house, terraced, with bay windows at the front of the property. It had three large rooms upstairs and a small washroom. Downstairs, there were another three large rooms and a scullery. At that time, there was no bath in the washroom and the lavatory for both families was situated in the back garden. It was all right in the summer. In the dead of night or in the winter it was a different story. Talk about freeze the balls off a brass monkey.

After investing all their savings, Mum and Dad were left with very little money and a lot of worry. Fortunately, the house was still standing after the

1939-45 war. Dad was a part-time fireman during that time, and even years later, not once did I ever hear him speak about any of the terrible things that he saw. He was excluded from joining up in the forces because apart from being a fireman, he had a good job employed as a sheet metal worker, working on Spitfires. Most of the women had to work during the war, but if their husbands were at home, doing war work, like my Dad, they only had to work part-time. Mum, together with some of the local women, worked in an ammunitions factory, doing various jobs, including making ammunition boxes. It was hard for everyone.

Auntie Eileen, my mother's sister, who was five years younger, met and fell in love with a sailor, Keith Walker, whom she later married. They had met during the war, whilst she was on holiday in Northampton, staying with my Nan's sister, Aunt Ag and her daughter Gladys. Being cousins and both coming from the same part of the country, Eileen and Gladys spent a lot of time together and were both interested in similar activities. Gladys at that time had a boyfriend, Fred, who was in the navy and when he came home on leave he bought his friend Keith with him.

Keith's family originally came from a small fishing village, Rosehearty, near Fraserburgh, Scotland. According to the stories that were told, when his family split up, when he was a child, he was placed in the care of Barnardo's, which was rather sad. However, to cut a long story short, as soon as he was old enough, he joined the Royal Navy and whilst on board ship, he made friends with Fred Peabody. Consequently, when Fred took him home to Northampton that day, and he was introduced to Eileen, there was no turning back.

Eileen married Keith when she was only seventeen

years of age and they set up home in a small flat, not far from where my Nan lived in Tottenham, North London. After only being together for a short time Keith had to return to his ship.

"I didn't want him to go back," Eileen said to her friend. "For all I know he is going to be away for months."

Days grew into weeks and Eileen began to feel increasingly tired. What with working full time and getting the flat sorted out, she was exhausted.

"I'd make myself an appointment with the doctor if I were you my girl," Pop, her father said, when he saw her that evening. "You look all in."

Eileen already had suspicions that she was pregnant but hadn't said anything to anybody.

On visiting the doctor's, Eileen underwent some tests and when she returned to the surgery the following week, to confirm whether in fact she was pregnant, the doctor said. "Mrs Walker, the tests have shown that you are having a baby. Come and see me again on Friday and I will make arrangements for you to go to the clinic. In the meantime I want you to take things easy for a few days."

Eileen was in a complete state of shock.

"Thank you doctor," was all she could say.

Not sure whether to laugh or cry, all she knew was that she wanted to speak to her sister.

"Cis," she called out as she saw her sister coming out of the factory gates. "Cissy," she called, catching her breath.

"Whatever is the matter, Eileen?" Cis said, quite concerned. "Has something happened to Keith?"

"No," replied Eileen. "I went to the doctor's today and he told me I'm three months pregnant." I don't know what I'm going to do."

Some of the women coming out of the factory knew Eileen, and overheard what she had said. "Congratulations," one of the women said, "Don't worry, you'll be all right."

"This calls for a celebration," said another. "Are you coming over the Park Hotel tonight for a drink?"

"Cis, that's a good idea," said Flo, one of the factory girls. "If you and Bert come over the pub tonight, bring Eileen with you. We can do with an excuse to have a booze-up."

"Blimey, since when have you lot needed an excuse?" Cis answered.

Before Cis had a chance to say anymore, the siren went off. For a moment everybody stood perfectly still just looking at each other. The next minute they started running for their homes or making their way to the air raid shelters.

Bill, the air raid warden, was a kind gentleman. Not only did he do his job working for the civil defence, he was also a good friend to a lot of people. Very often he passed on messages, letting people know whether other members of their family were safe. He would arrange for help to be given when necessary and as far as the older people were concerned, he would reassure them in times of trouble. There was one old lady, Lucy, who refused to go in the air raid shelter.

"Leave me alone," she said. "If those buggers are going to get me, I'd rather be where I'm comfortable."

On this occasion, Bill left her sitting in the armchair by the fire, doing her knitting.

"Are you all right?" Bill asked.

"Yes," she replied. "I've made myself a flask of cocoa, so I'll be all right."

By the morning, there was more than one family that had been bombed out. Lives were lost and many people were injured.

"Bloody jerries," said Lucy, when Bill called in to see her the following day. "They all want shooting."

As Bill shut the door behind him, he couldn't help but have a little grin to himself.

From what my Mum has told me since, the siren would go off nearly every evening just as it was getting dark. On many occasions, after having tea, she would stand at the gate waiting for the siren, Moaning Minnie, to go off. Armed with an overnight bag in one hand and insurance policies in the other, she would run all the way to my Nan's house in Asplins Road and take cover in the air raid shelter, which Nan and Pop had in their back garden. On one occasion, when my Dad was with her, they were running down Shelbourne Road on the way to my Nan's when Dad shouted.

"Quick Cis, get down."

Without saying another word, my Dad pushed her through someone's garden gate and she fell in a puddle.

"Oh Bert," she said after getting soaked through. "Look at the state of me."

She laughed about it afterwards, but at the time, with bombs overhead, she was scared stiff.

Fortunately, when Nan and Pop got bombed out, nobody was in the house. My Mum and Dad had only recently had an Anderson shelter installed in their garden at Willoughby Lane, and they were making themselves comfortable for the night. As on other occasions, in the back garden of Asplins Road, Nan, Pop and Auntie Eileen were having a nightcap in the air raid shelter before settling down and trying to get some sleep. With all the noise going on around them it was difficult, but nobody dare come out until the 'all clear' sound was heard.

When morning came and Nan and Pop saw that their house had been bombed, they were upset and tears were shed but they counted themselves lucky because unlike some families, they were all very much alive. People in the area came to help and it wasn't too long before the authorities found them another place to live. As their children, Cis and Eileen were now married and no longer living at home, Nan and Pop were allocated a one bedroom flat in Park Lane opposite to where Auntie Eileen lived.

Dora, the lady who lived upstairs, introduced herself the day that they moved in and before very long, she was being treated like one of the family. From what Dora told them, her husband John, was a sergeant in the Royal Air Force and was stationed in Oban, Argyllshire. Whatever thoughts my Nan and Pop had of the young man who was married to the blonde upstairs, they were quite different from the man behind the uniform. Nobody in the family was prepared for the day that Johnny Newman came home on leave.

It seemed that during the war, when nobody knew if there was going to be a tomorrow, people would let their hair down and they really enjoyed themselves. Sometimes when things were quiet, the locals would get together in the pub and have a singsong, especially if Frank the piano player was there.

"Play 'Pack up your troubles' Frank," Pop said, setting up another pint of beer on top of the piano. "Go on, just for our Eileen."

"Thanks mate," said Frank. After supping his beer, he began to play. The more he played, the more songs people sang. The pub was packed, and by closing time, the majority of people left, feeling as if they'd had a really good time.

The flat that Eileen and Keith rented was looking really nice now. Even though there wasn't a lot of money to spare, relatives and friends had managed to get some nice pieces of second hand furniture for them. Her grandmother had given her some material to make up curtains and chair covers. Even Pop had helped out by doing little jobs.

"You've got a nice little place here," said Cis when she called in to see her sister that afternoon.

"I am trying to get everything sorted out by the time the baby comes," Eileen replied. "I just hope I hear from Keith soon."

Over the next few months, Eileen's legs had started to swell and she was beginning to feel really poorly. No longer working in the machine shop, she had more time for herself and would often go across the road to where her parents lived. Sometimes, she would have a meal with them and spend the rest of the time sewing or reading the local newspaper.

"Have you heard from Keith yet?" Pop asked when he saw Eileen looking a bit depressed.

"Yes, I heard from him yesterday," Eileen replied. "He is hoping to get leave soon."

"That's good," said Pop, quietly. "With a bit of luck, he will be home when you have that baby of yours."

By half past seven that evening, Eileen found herself falling asleep in the armchair.

"I hope you don't mind, but I'm going to turn in now," she said. "An early night will do me good. I feel all in."

"You'll feel better after a good nights sleep," her mother said. "Why don't you stay here for the night?"

"Thanks Mum."

Within a short space of time the camp bed was made

up under the stairs, and Eileen was getting ready for bed.

"You mind how you go my girl," said Pop as he saw her knock her knee on the corner of the bed.

"Goodnight," she said as she kissed him on the cheek. "Goodnight."

Friday morning was unusually busy in the clinic. Eileen had been sitting in the waiting room for what seemed like an hour, and all there was to do was sit and read the dog eared magazines that were on the little coffee table in the corner, or chat to the other expectant mothers.

"I hate this hanging about," Eileen said.

"Yes, I feel the same. I've been sitting here since half past nine," replied the lady sitting next to her. "I hope they hurry up."

Another few minutes went by before the nurse came over to her and said, "Mrs Walker, will you come this way please."

After having a sample of her urine taken and being pulled about whilst being examined, she was relieved to hear that everything was all right.

"There is no need to worry, Mrs Walker," the doctor said. "The baby is nicely positioned and we can hear a good heart beat."

With the examination over, Eileen got dressed and walked out into the sunshine. It was a relief to know that everything was all right. As she hadn't been feeling well over the last few weeks, she was worried that the baby would be born before the due date.

"How did you get on at the clinic?" Cis asked when she called in to see her sister after work.

Eileen made Cis a cup of tea and told her all about it.

"I knew you were worried," Cis said. "At least now

that you know everything is all right, you can put your mind at rest."

The following weekend, Cis and Bert were having a cuddle in bed when they were disturbed by a loud noise. A man was banging on the window of the front door with his fist.

"Wait a minute, Cis called out as she hurriedly put on her dressing gown. "Who is it?"

Before Cis opened the front door, she took a peek through the net curtains to see who it was and recognized that the man standing on the doorstep was one of Eileen's neighbours, Mr Calvert.

"What is it?" said Cis as she saw the serious look on Mr Calvert's face.

"I've got some bad news for you I'm afraid," Mr Calvert replied in a very sombre tone. "It's Eileen. She's been taken bad."

"Give me a few minutes and I'll get dressed," Cissie said. "You had better come in and wait."

By the time Cis arrived at the house, it was obvious that Eileen's baby was due to be born. Something was terribly wrong though. Why had Nanny Edwards, been sent for!

"There's nothing you can do. Just make sure there's plenty of hot water and don't let anyone come into the bedroom."

You could hear Eileen screaming through the walls and then there was silence. Nan and her mother in law, Nanny Edwards, came into the living room and explained to the family that Eileen had given birth to a baby boy. The sad thing was that it had died inside her. "The baby had started to decompose." Nan said. "It was all shriveled up and black in colour."

What was upsetting was that once Eileen had given birth, the baby was discarded like some unwanted piece of meat and placed in a brown paper bag behind the armchair. Somebody from the authorities collected it and because the baby hadn't drawn breath, he hadn't been given a name. There was no funeral and from what I understand, was placed in another persons coffin before burial. For a young mother who had gone through all the experience of childbirth, that was cruel.

Auntie Eileen never did get over the experience, especially after being told that she couldn't have any more children. The question that remained unanswered was: why did it happen? After all, when she had attended the clinic, it was confirmed that the baby was all right. Was Eileen just another casualty of the war?

CHAPTER TWO

Many people wanted to forget the atrocious things that happened during April 1945. The war was coming to an end but still the fighting went on. All over Britain families were waiting for news of their loved ones and Mrs Smith was no exception.

Mrs Smith's daughter Jane was going through her own private war, not knowing what was going to happen after her baby was born. Too much had happened to her too soon, and now, as she lay with her legs wide open, she listened only to the voice at the foot of the bed, "Push." Exhausted, her mind no longer in turmoil, she gave birth to a little girl, Frances.

Frances came into the world a fighter. Her little hands screwed up into tiny fists, she kicked and yelled so loud as if to say to the world "Well I'm here. Against all the odds I made it. I'm alive."

Nobody knew what was going to happen tomorrow, let alone next week. At the time, Jane didn't even know whether she would be keeping her baby. A decision had to be made. Was Frances going to be adopted?

The tiny bundle of life wrapped up in the hospital blanket was oblivious to all the commotion around her. Warm and content, Frances slept through until tea time, the nurses keeping a watchful eye on her and all the other babies in the nursery.

It was so quiet you could hear the clock on the wall ticking. Jane was exhausted and her face was red and puffy where she had been crying. Mr Brewer, the social worker, had sat with her for over an hour and because Jane was an unmarried mother, he explained that because of her circumstances, it may be difficult for her to keep the baby. "Arrangements can be made for adoptive parents to be found most suitable to the babies needs," he told her.

Mr Brewer gently closed the door behind him and for a few moments Jane was motionless. Staring at the door handle, she thought, 'Why me? Why does everything happen to me?'

For what may have been the last time, Jane washed, fed and held the baby in her arms. Now, with every ounce of strength she had left, she made her way down the corridor to the nursery. The time had come for her to say goodnight.

What happened to Jane when she left the hospital nobody really knows? What is on record is that on 8th May 1945 Frances Eirowen was registered as having been born in the sub-district of Paddington West on 24th April 1945 and arrangements were being made for her to be adopted. By September of that year, the adoption order was signed and no two people could have been happier when only sixteen days later Cis and Bert Pink were the proud parents of their adopted daughter, whom they called Sandra Denise. Yes, I was that little girl.

What really happened during those five months? Did Jane Smith really exist or was the name she used a pseudonym? What part of the country did she come from? Was she Irish or Welsh? Who knows the answer to these questions? In fact, who knew anything about the lady who lived in Bathurst Gardens?

Cis and Bert had been married for nearly six years when I came into their lives. Cissie wanted a little boy and planned to call him Peter. Fate however, had other plans.

From what the family said, when Cis and Bert went into the children's home to view the babies, Bert took a peek into a baby's cot. The baby looking up at him had the most appealing eyes. As he extended his hand to straighten the blanket around her, she grabbed hold of his little finger and wouldn't let go. He just couldn't take his eyes of the little girl with a mass of thick black hair. He was smitten. "We'll have her Cis," he said. "We'll take her home."

The house in Willoughby Lane was full of happiness the day Cis and Bert bought me home. Nan and Pop were there with Auntie Eileen and Uncle Keith. It was like Christmas. Knowing that his daughter Cissie was going to adopt a little baby, Pop had arranged for a teddy bear to be made some weeks earlier and with everything on ration, you can imagine the trouble he went to, to make sure the teddy bear was ready on time.

Over the years, poor old 'Ted' as we called the teddy bear, took some beatings. He was dragged round the garden. Went for rides in the pram and even went with the family on a bus journey to Petticoat Lane. Red buttons were replaced for his eyes, the family dog had chewed his right ear and eventually he had to go to a dolls hospital because his arm had become detached from his body. When 'Ted' finally came home, he wasn't the same. His arms and legs still moved independently but he now looked at you with soulful eyes and he had put on weight.

One hundred and thirty four miles from Tottenham and twenty nine years later, in a little village called High Littleton in Avon, 'Ted' found himself in the bed of another little girl who was adopted. If a teddy bear could talk, I expect by now he would have told another little girl or boy all about the adventures that he'd had.

I don't really know what was different about that summer afternoon in High Littleton. Whilst out the front garden with my second husband, Norman, up to my elbows in dirt and horse manure, a man walked by with his little girl.

The little girl was about three years of age with long golden curls. Something she had seen in the garden obviously held her attention because she didn't take her eyes of us. In fact, it was quite unnerving seeing a small child staring at you through the wrought iron gate.

"Come on little one," her father said, reaching out for her hand. "It's rude to stand and stare."

Whatever the little girl's father said, or did, she still gripped onto the gate and just wouldn't let go.

The stranger looked at us and apologized for his little girl's behaviour.

"I'm sorry," he said, "I don't know what has come over her. She's not normally like this."

"Don't worry," said Norman. "I think it must be the dog that she is interesting in."

We hadn't been in the area long and didn't know very many people, so I took the opportunity of speaking to the gentleman.

"Excuse me." I said. "Can you tell us where Midsomer Norton is please? We only moved here recently and apart from going to Bristol every day to work, we haven't been to many places."

"Yes," he replied. "It will only take about 10 minutes to get there in the car."

"Jess," Norman called, when he saw our dog trying to scramble through the hedge.

Hearing my husband's voice, our little Yorkshire terrier came running over, wagging her tail. The look on the child's face was a picture when Jess rolled over on her back to have her tummy tickled.

"I thought it might be the dog that was interesting you," Norman said bending down speaking to the little girl. "Do you like dogs?"

The little girl didn't answer. Instead, she turned to her father and held onto his trouser leg.

"She's terribly shy," he said, lifting her up into his arms.

After we introduced ourselves, we stood chatting for quite a long time and during the conversation, we discovered that Midsomer Norton was only about five miles away. The gentleman not only gave us directions how to get there but also recommended a nice restaurant, Jan's Kitchen, where they served good steaks.

"Thanks," Norman said. "We might take a ride there later on."

So as not to appear rude, I excused myself while I went indoors to wash my hands and when I returned Mr Ryder and Norman were still engrossed in conversation. Ken Ryder was a kind gentleman and from what he was saying, both he and his wife, Barbara, adopted their little girl Sally when she was only a few months old. They both had good teaching jobs and had moved back into the area when Ken got a posting at the University of Bristol.

Looking again at Ken, you could form a mental picture of him teaching a lot of students. The man had a kind face. His brown eyes were alive and friendly and when he smiled, his whole face lit up. However, I am sure that in the classroom, he could be quite assertive.

For some reason, it seemed only right that 'Ted', who had been sitting upstairs on the dressing table for so long, should have another lease of life. As if by telepathy, both Norman and I had the same thoughts. Quietly, without the little girl hearing, Norman whispered to me. "Why don't we give her the teddy bear?"

I didn't say anything, just nodded in agreement.

"Before you go," Norman said, looking at the little girl. "We have got something for you."

I made my way upstairs, to our bedroom, to get 'Ted' and I was not sorry to let the little girl have him. He had given me and other children a lot of pleasure during my lifetime and I knew in my heart of hearts that he would have a good home.

"Here you are," I said, showing the little girl the teddy bear. "Here is a little present for you."

Sally, the little girl, held the bear tightly to her chest and gave her father a big smile. Then they were gone.

Whilst we were in the garden, a few months later, we saw Mr Ryder and he told us that Sally took the bear to bed with her every night. I was pleased. At long last 'Ted' was making someone else happy.

CHAPTER THREE

As both Cis and her sister, Eileen, didn't have any
children, when I came into their lives in nineteen forty
five, there was a lot of love to go round. I had the best
that they could offer. Even though money was short,
the family gave me a good start in life, and more than
anything, I was wanted. Not only was I the only child,
I was also the only niece and my Nan and Pop's only
grandchild. As I was growing up, you would have
thought that I was the luckiest child around.

The first memory I had was when I was nearly three
years of age sitting on top of a wash bag being pushed
in a pram by my Nan. Whatever the weather, Nan
would call round to the house before Mum went to
work and we would spend the days together. Every
Monday, Nan would collect our washing and we would
go to Bromley Road laundry. Even after I went to
school, during the holidays, I would ask Nan if I could
go with her.

The laundry was a meeting place for all the
housewives in the area and seeing them working in
their floral aprons with their hair tucked up in
headscarves was quite a scene.

With all the machines going at the same time, and
the women gossiping, the noise was very loud. I was
fascinated. Blue bags would go into the coppers to get
the sheets and pillowcases extra white and sometimes
Nan would let me stand on a chair by the deep sinks.
Using a washboard I would rub the collars and cuffs of
the shirts before they went into the machines. I could
barely hold the washing soap in my hand, the bar was
so big, but I felt quite grown up helping my Nan.

To this day I still love the smell of freshly laundered

linen, especially nice clean sheets on the bed.

Sometimes, I would go with Nan to get the shopping at Plaistow's in Park Lane and often she would buy a bag of mixed broken biscuits for a few pennies. When we got home I would sort out all the pink wafers and eat them before anyone else got a look in. "You are a naughty girl," Nan would say, but I knew she didn't mind really.

We were in Plaistow's on one occasion and Mr Plaistow asked me if I wanted to see some kittens.

"Yes please," I said.

He took me through to the stockroom at the back of the shop and in one of the boxes there were five small balls of fur. The kittens were so young that they didn't even have their eyes open. I picked up one to stroke it but the kitten's mother was not very happy about me holding her baby, so I gently put the kitten back in the box with the others.

"When they get bigger, can I take one home?" I asked Mr Plaistow.

"Only if your Mum and Dad say you can," he replied with a grin.

No sooner had Bert, my Dad, got home from work that night I said: "Can I have a kitten Dad?" I was so excited. "Please."

"Give us a chance," he said. "Let's get my coat off first."

Some weeks later I went back to Plaistow's with my Dad to collect the kitten that I'd chosen, but unfortunately we couldn't keep it.

"That's a wild cat," my Dad told me. "His ears are too big and it's not fair to keep the animal confined to a small flat when he had been used to running free."

The kitten had already scratched me badly and had jumped out from under the chair and fastened itself round my Mum's leg. Not only had she been scratched, but also the kitten had sunk its teeth into her ankle. Ouch!

I was upset when we took the kitten back to Mr Plaistow but Fluff was quite happy to see his brother and sisters again. A matter of minutes after we let him out of the box he was chasing the other kittens round the stockroom. They were having a wonderful time.

"I'm sorry Sandra," Mum said when we got home. "We just couldn't keep him."

Dad tried to pacify me and promised that I would have another kitten one day.

One bright Sunday morning my Dad asked Mum if I could go with him to Petticoat Lane. Dad didn't have a car in those days, so we went on two long bus rides to get there. Dad helped me up the stairs on the big bus and I sat by the window.

"Look Dad!" I said. "You can see right over that lady's garden wall."

"Yes," he replied. "You can see a lot more sitting upstairs on the bus."

Pointing my finger in the direction of where some children were playing hopscotch, I said: "Look Dad!"

"Shush!" he said, giving me a nudge with his elbow. "It's rude to point your finger at people."

I sat quiet for the rest of the journey taking in everything I saw. There were people digging their gardens. More children were playing bat and ball and one man was letting his pigeons out of his pigeon loft.

"Look Dad," I said, not being able to contain myself any longer. "He's got pigeons like you."

When we got to our destination we got off the bus and made our way to Middlesex Street.

"Do you fancy a bacon sandwich?" Dad said. "I know where there's a nice little café."

Sure enough, just around the corner we saw some people coming out of the café and one man recognised my Dad.

"Morning Bert," he said. "I see you've got your little girl with you today." Looking at me, he raised his cap. "Good morning, young lady."

Dad stopped and spoke to the man for a few minutes. "See you later Bill," Dad said as he took me by the hand and led me inside the café to where it was nice and warm.

"Dad," I called out, not liking a strange man who was walking past the window wearing a long flowing robe and had feathers sticking out of his hair. The man was shouting something out loud but I couldn't understand what he was saying. I was frightened. "Who is he?" I asked. "What was he saying?"

Dad saw the look on my face and said, "Don't worry. He won't hurt you. I expect we'll see him again later on."

Dad explained that the man was a racing tipster and was down the lane every week. "That's Prince Monolulu," Dad said.

Apparently, Prince Monolulu was quite a character and we saw him a few times after that.

"I've got a horse," the man would shout. "Anybody want a horse?"

We sat for a little while watching people go past the window of the café when we heard someone call from the kitchen.

"Who ordered two bacon sandwiches and two teas?"

Dad acknowledged that they were for us and a young waitress brought them over to our table.

"Here you are." Dad said, passing me a serviette.

If you didn't know any different you would have

thought I hadn't eaten for a week. Lashings of butter had been put on the bread and the sandwich had so much bacon in, I had a job to finish it. I took a sip of tea from my mug and it was so hot that I nearly spilt some.

"Careful," Dad said, taking the mug from my hand. "Watch you don't burn yourself."

I was thoroughly enjoying myself. It was nice being out on my own with my Dad. He was telling me funny stories that made me laugh.

"See you next week," the owner of the café called out as we were leaving.

Petticoat Lane gets ever so busy on a Sunday and this Sunday was no exception. There were lots of stalls where crowds gathered but I was too small to see everything that was going on. The next thing I knew, Dad lifted me onto his shoulders and we watched a stallholder doing a juggling act with cups and saucers. How he managed to throw a whole tea service up in the air and catch it without breaking anything I don't know.

People were buying lots of things at knock down prices on the market. There were people selling everything. Clothes, linen, household items, china and glass, tools and in one part of the lane, Club Row, they were selling birds and animals.

Dad had some business to attend to at the bird stall and he bought two pigeons for half a crown each. He also looked at some goldfinches and canaries.

"What's that bird doing in the cage Joe?" Dad asked the fat man, pointing to a small bird that was making a high pitched noise.

"Which one are you on about mate?" Joe said as he came out from behind a stack of cages.

I knew Dad was cross because his bottom lip was

twitching.

"Be a good girl and go and have a look at those puppies while I talk to Joe a minute," he said, looking directly at me. I knew by the way he looked at me that I had to keep out of the way for a little while. Still keeping an eye on me, Dad waited until I'd made my way to where the puppies were kept in a small enclosure and then he turned his head and continued talking to Joe. The next thing I saw was that Dad was holding a small bird in his hand. Releasing his grip, the bird flew up into the air.

I was quite happy looking at the puppies. Some were nervous and stayed huddled together in the corner, but the others were inquisitive and enjoyed being stroked and having a fuss made of them. I wasn't too sure of one though because he tried to chew my fingers. His teeth were ever so sharp.

It wasn't too long before Dad came over to where I was standing.

"Come on Sandra," he said. "We'll have to make our way back now, otherwise your mother will be wondering what has happened to us."

"What have you got in that box Dad?" I said to him as we made our way back to the bus stop.

Whilst we were waiting for the bus to arrive, he opened the small oblong box he had in his hand and showed me some watches.

"What are you going to do with those?" I asked him. "They are all broken."

"I only paid a couple of bob for them," he replied. "By the time I have finished with them, they will be working as good as new and I can sell them for twenty five bob each. That way, I make a profit and it pays for my pigeon corn and tobacco."

I was forever asking questions when I was a child

and wanted to know all there was to know about everything. I drove my parents mad when I kept asking questions. 'Why?' 'What's that for?' 'Who's that?' You could say that I was being nosey but I had an inquisitive mind.

"Dad, I said to him. "Why did you let that bird out of the cage?" He got quite agitated at this stage and explained that birds that are born in the wild should not be kept in cages. What had made Dad angry was that the owner of the bird stall, whom Dad was having a conversation with earlier, had a wild bird in one of the cages. Because Dad knew all about birds, he agreed to pay Joe a few shillings just for the privilege of letting the bird go.

I knew my Dad was a rascal, but it was only when I grew older that I realised how street wise he was. Financially, compared to some of my school friends, we were quite poor but when it came to making a few extra shillings, he knew all the tricks of the trade. I can remember that on one occasion, he sold some pigeons to the bird stall when we went to Club Row, knowing full well that as soon as the new owner let them out of their pigeon loft, they would fly back home.

Over the years, Dad often took me to Petticoat Lane and Club Row and sometimes he would buy something for my Mum. On this particular day my grandfather, Pop, came with us and he gave me half-a-crown to spend, which was a lot of money in those days.

Dad managed to get Mum the marcasite watch that she wanted for her birthday and Pop bought himself a pair of new boots for work.

"Before we go back," said Pop, looking across to where Dad and I were standing. "I want to call into Tubby Isaacs to get some jellied eels. Do you want some prawns for your tea Sandra?" he asked me.

"Yes please. Are you going to get half a pint of winkles as well?" I said with a cheeky grin. As far as Pop was concerned, I could do no wrong! He would have given me the world if he could.

"Do you want to get anything else with the rest of your pocket money?" Dad asked, as we passed the market trader selling bankrupt stock.

I don't know why I did it, but just at that moment the man at the back of the lorry was saying in a loud voice. "Five tins of Elastoplasts'. Not the price of four tins. Not the price of three tins. How much? Five tins for the price of two."

Without thinking, I put my hand in my pocket and gave the man the money for them. Needless to day, when they were opened later in the day, there were only two or three plasters in each tin.

"Dad," this can't be right."

"That will teach you my girl," he said, after looking from my shocked expression into the contents of the tins. "You have got to remember that in this world, you only get what you pay for."

We all had a good laugh about it afterwards.

My dad was a hard working man and always kept his word. When the time was right, he took me back to Club Row and we chose a kitten together. I was thrilled. I couldn't believe it.

"What shall we call him Dad?" I said as we set off for the journey home on the bus. After various names we decided that Timmy was a good name. "Timmy." I said out loud. "Dad, I like that name."

We got back home just as Mum was dishing up the dinner. My favourite was roast beef and Yorkshire pudding but today we were having steak and kidney pie.

"Come on you two," Mum called from the landing.

"If you had been any longer your dinner would have been spoiled."

I knew we weren't too late because Billy Cotton's Band Show was still playing on the radio. Whilst Mum was pouring the gravy over our dinners, Dad gave me a knowing wink and took Timmy out of the cat box and gave him some milk.

"Oh no Bert, you haven't got her another kitten!" Mum said as she saw what was going on. "You know what happened to the last one."

"Cissie," Dad said as he put his arm around Mum's shoulder. "It will be nice for Sandra to have an animal around the place. Besides, you said yourself that it would be a good idea to have another cat, especially after you saw the mouse run behind the gas stove.

"Eat your dinner, before it gets cold," was all she had to say.

Believe me, within a few hours it was my Mum who was playing with the kitten. Not only had she given him something to play with, she had opened up a tin of red salmon for our tea, and given him some as well. Talk about being spoiled.

Timmy grew up to be an alley cat. He may have been scarred from fighting, his white coat with grey and black markings may have lost its sheen, but he was my friend. I shared more secrets with that cat than anyone else on earth. Timmy stayed with us for about nine years, until one day he decided not to come home anymore. Whether he got run over on the railway line at the back of our house or whether he found another home, I don't know. All I know is that I missed him.

CHAPTER FOUR

The one thing that did give me a lot of pleasure when I was a child was dancing. At every opportunity, when music was being played on the wireless, I would prance around, swinging my arms and legs. Sometimes, I would pretend I was Margot Fonteyn the ballet dancer and in my imagination, I was pirouetting on stage. In reality, I was in the corner of the living room, barefoot, dressed like a tomboy.

"Get your slippers on," Mum said. "You'll catch your death of cold running around on that cold lino."

It had been agreed by the family that because of my interest in dancing, I could join the local dancing class and go just one evening a week.

"Well," said Pop when I got home from the first visit that Monday evening. "How did you get on?"

"I loved it," I replied excitedly. "Madame said that if I am going to join, I have to take my own ballet and tap shoes. Can I?"

"We'll have to see about that," Pop said, looking at my Mum. "It's no good us paying out good money for ballet and tap shoes if she's going to get fed up with it after a couple of weeks."

"No I won't," I said, raising my voice slightly, as I interrupted their conversation. "I like dancing."

By the time the next Monday came, I set off to the dance class with a bag containing my new tap shoes. I felt really pleased that my parents were going to let me do something on my own. Mum walked me to the hall where the lessons were being held and after going through the big oak doors and paying my subs, she left me and promised to return at half past seven to take me home. I wasn't on my own for long. Another girl,

28

Linda Hargrave, spoke to me.

"Hello," she said. "I saw you here last week. You've decided to join us then?"

"Yes," I replied.

Within the next few months, I'd learned a lot of dance steps and passed an audition to be in the next concert. I was really enthusiastic and when I told my parents, they were really pleased for me.

"Mum," I said when she picked me up Monday evening. "Madame wants to see you."

"What for?" she said. "You haven't been a naughty girl have you?"

"No I haven't, I said indignantly as I pulled out a crumpled piece of paper from my pocket. "I've got a note here for you. Madame wants to see you about getting me a pair of ballet shoes."

"We'll have to talk to your Dad when we get home." She answered.

Mum went to see Madame when we next had a lesson and it was obvious from what Madame said that I would definitely be in the next concert. I was thrilled that I'd been chosen but nervous at the same time.

The tap dance routines were difficult to remember without the music being played but after a lot of hard work and many rehearsals we were ready. With the help of our parents and a lot of other people, we had all managed to get the standard costume to wear on stage. We all wore a white silk blouse with the name of our dance class embroidered on it, a red silk skirt that was very short, white ankle socks and red tap-dancing shoes. The dress rehearsal was the first time we saw ourselves all dressed up and it was quite a thrill. We were all made up with a little lipstick and some powder and I even had rouge put on my face.

The day of the concert arrived and we were all very

nervous. Those of us who had long hair had our hair plaited and clipped securely to each side of our heads so that when we did the dance routine, our hair wouldn't get in our eyes.

"Girls," Madame said in a loud voice. "During the interval as we only have fifteen minutes to change, could we please be as quiet as possible. I don't want anybody talking."

Looking directly at me, she said: "If I hear anybody giggling or shouting then they will be sent home."

Madame was very strict, so we knew that she meant what she said. The music was being played and we all found our place on stage.

"Now, remember what I said," she whispered.

Linda Hargrave, being our leader, was at the front of the stage and the rest of us were in three lines behind her. We knew that as soon as we heard the introduction to 'On the Good Ship, Lollipop' we were to take a deep breath and concentrate on our dance steps.

All together there were sixteen of us on stage including Linda and for the few minutes that we were there, each and every one of us did our very best.

"Shuffle, hop, back step," Madame whispered from the wings. "Forward, two, three, four."

We did so well that at the end of our routine, we got a loud applause. It was magic.

"Well done," said Madame as we moved off stage after taking a curtain call. "Well done."

Once we were off stage, we were all so excited that it was difficult to stay quiet.

"Shush!" one of the stagehands said, putting his forefinger to his lips. "Please be quiet," he whispered.

When the announcement came that there was a fifteen minute interval, to me, it was as though the television had been turned up. We all started talking ten to the dozen. Giggles and laughter filled the air and when we were all given a drink of squash and a packet of crisps to eat, you could just barely hear the crackle of paper as we opened our crisps.

"Quickly," said Madame as she entered the dressing room. "Those of you who are on stage after the interval, I want you to get changed now. The rest of you, please gather up your things and make your way to the back of the hall."

There were ten of us remaining, including Linda, to change and get ready for the next act. In the dance routine, I had to dress up as a ragamuffin. Instead of lipstick and powder, someone made me up with what looked like boot polish smudged on my face. My hair was brushed and clipped close to my head and my Dad had lent me his works cap to wear. Instead of tap shoes, I had to go barefoot and someone splashed my feet with some liquid that looked like mud.

"Come on girls," one of the teachers said. "It's time you were all ready."

As quietly as possible we all made our way to the side of the stage to wait for our cue when suddenly my mind went blank. We'd rehearsed this routine many times before but suddenly I had stage fright. My face must have given me away because Linda asked me if I was okay.

"Don't worry," she said when I told her what was wrong. "You'll be all right once you hear the music."

Fortunately, when the curtain went up, I was at the back of the stage. It took all my concentration to remember what I had to do next and I couldn't take my eyes of the other girls' feet.

"Back row to the front," Madame prompted from the wings. "One, two, three, four," she whispered.

I remembered what to do next. Suddenly it all

became clear and my nerves disappeared. At last, I was beginning to enjoy myself. As I went to the front of the stage for the second time, I lowered my head as instructed by the choreographer and just at that moment, the cap that I was wearing came off my head landing on the stage. Whoops.

Without giving it another thought, in time to the music, I retrieved the cap with my right hand and deftly put it back on top of my head. No one said a word. I returned to my position at the back of the stage and breathed a sigh of relief.

"Keep in line," I heard someone say from the wings.

Loud clapping filled our ears at the end of the dance and we all took a bow. I was so embarrassed about what happened that my face was the colour of a bright tomato.

"Trust you," said one of the girls when I came off stage. "For a minute there, I thought you were going to fall over."

"Never mind," said Madame sympathetically. "The audience probably thought it was part of the routine. Now quickly children, I want you all to get changed. Remember, I want you all to be as quiet as possible."

In the dressing room a few minutes later, we could hardly move. There were clothes and shoes all over the place. How we managed to clean ourselves up in the small space there was, I don't know.

"I can't find my shoes," said one of the girls.

"Where's my skirt?" said another.

Eventually, with the help from a few adults, we had cleaned ourselves up and gathered most of our belongings together. It wasn't until we got into the main hall that someone told me that I still had a large black mark on my face.

"Come here," my Mum said when she saw me. You

look like a dead end kid."

I didn't say a word but was embarrassed when she proceeded to wipe my face after licking a clean hanky.

"Don't Mum," I said. "I'll go and wash my face properly."

As all the seats had been taken in the main hall, those of us who wanted to see the rest of the concert were allowed to go upstairs and watch from the balcony.

"Can I go upstairs Mum?" I said, looking at her with my big blue eyes.

"Yes," she said. "Only if you stay with your friends and wait for me to come and get you after the concert."

"Don't worry," one of the teachers said. "We'll look after her until then."

I managed to squeeze on the bench with some of the other girls and we thoroughly enjoyed ourselves. The concert didn't finish until after ten o'clock but it was an enjoyable evening and it was nice being with my friends. At the end of the concert, we all made our way on stage for the Finale and sang 'God Save the King'. Madame thanked us for doing our best.

"Have a nice Christmas girls," she said, as we were getting ready to leave. "I hope to see you all next year when the new term starts."

"Goodnight Linda," I called out, making my way to the front entrance where Mum and Dad were waiting. "Goodnight."

"You must be the girl that lost her hat," Linda's brother, John, said cheekily.

Embarrassed, I could feel my cheeks burning.

"Goodnight Pinky," he said with a laugh.

I wasn't at all pleased. But twelve years later, I would be married to him.

CHAPTER FIVE

I liked Friday nights - Armani nights we called them. It was the night that Dad bought us home sweets after he got paid. After we'd had our tea, which was usually fish and chips, we would settle down for the evening listening to the wireless. Mum would light the copper and when the water was hot enough she would fill up the galvanised bath, which when not in use, was kept hanging on a hook in the garden, and give me a good scrub.

It's difficult to imagine now, in this day and age but in the nineteen fifties, it was heavenly sitting in the bath by a roaring coal fire.

"When was the last time you washed your neck?" Mum said harshly.

"Ouch! I've got soap in my eyes," I would cry out when she washed my hair.

"Oh don't be such a baby. I could have washed ten kids while I've been seeing to you," was all she had to say.

I must admit that washing my hair was a chore in itself. My hair was so long that when it was brushed every night, I could sit on it.

With every part of my body cleaned and scrubbed Mum would pour some more hot water into the bath and let me play for a little while with all the bubbles. Sometimes, she would sit on the floor by the side of the bath and cupping her hands around the soapsuds, she would blow really big bubbles and they would float in the air.

"Time to get out now," Mum said, throwing a large towel round my shoulders. "I want to get your hair dry before you go to bed."

Mum towel dried my hair and for a little while I sat by the fire, reading my comic. At other times, I would help Mum sort out the old clothes to make rug mats. I would sit for ages with her, cutting up strips of material whilst she threaded the cloth with a latch hook, through pieces of sacking. Those mats, when completed, lasted for years.

"Come on Sandra," Mum said, once the clock on the mantelpiece had chimed eight o'clock. "It's bed time."

I knew tonight that it was no use arguing, because in the morning, I was going away for a few days with Nick and Dib.

"Who are Nick and Dib?" my friend, Christine, had asked when I told her.

The couple that were taking me away, I explained, lived in the flat above my Nan.

"Their real names are Dora and John Newman," I said. "I don't know why but close friends and family always call them Nick and Dib. I heard my Mum say that he's Old Nick the devil"

Whatever the reason, I was accepted by Dib as the child she never had and over the years, people often thought that Dib was my real Mum. Who knows?

When I got up the following morning, I was so excited about going away to Westcliff-on-Sea with Nick and Dib that I couldn't get my bag packed quick enough. I'd never been for a long ride in a car before, let alone stayed in a hotel. I remember once Mum and Dad took me to Margate in a charabanc and we stayed in a guesthouse for a few days. Apart from that, all I can remember is going on a train to Northampton to see my Mum's cousin, Auntie Rose, and her family. You can imagine what a thrill it was for me, knowing that I was going to travel in a car. I thought that Nick must be rich, because I heard that only rich people had cars and televisions.

"What kind of car is it, Nick?" Dad asked when he saw the car the following morning, outside the house where my Nan lived.

"It's a Jowett Javelin," Nick replied, showing off.

Dad was genuinely interested in the car and for the next quarter of an hour they were discussing specifications, aerodynamics and such like. Not being able to understand a word of what the conversation was about, I went indoors and spoke to my Nan for a little while.

"Here you are Sandra," Nan said, when she saw me, offering me a slice of bread and dripping.

"No thank you," I said. "I had my breakfast before I came out."

Nan fussed over me like an old mother hen and I was glad when I could make my excuses and go upstairs with Dib.

From the day that I could talk, Noonan was my childish interpretation of Dib's surname, Newman. Today, teasingly, I called from the bottom of the stairs.

"Can I come up there Noonan?"

Hearing my voice, Dib looked over the top of the banisters and said: "Come on up if you want to, but we will be leaving in a minute."

A few minutes late, Nick appeared. "If you want a job, you can help me carry these things out to the car," he said.

"What's in the basket?" I asked being nosy.

"Dib had packed us up something for lunch," he replied. "It's quite a long drive and we thought it would be a good idea to stop and have something to eat on the way."

After giving my Nan a kiss on the cheek and saying

goodbye to my Dad, I settled in the back of the car but was rather quiet. I didn't know Nick very well, as he had only just been demobbed from the Royal Air Force and I found his manner rather brusque. Driving out of London towards Southend, it was nice seeing the countryside with all the animals in the fields. It was a shame that it had started to rain.

"You're quiet sitting in the back there," Nick said. "Are you all right?"

"I'm fine," I said.

If the truth was known, I hadn't had much sleep the night before and was feeling really tired. In fact, I had a job keeping my eyes open.

"We are over half way now," Nick said, looking at the signpost. "If you see a place to stop, give me a shout and we'll have a cuppa."

"That's a good idea, I need a pee as well," Dib said, lighting up another cigarette.

"How about you Pol. Do you want anything?"

It was nothing new being called by another name, other than Sandra. If Dib didn't call me Polly 'Opkins or Pol for short, Nick would call me Potty. To be honest, he continued to call me Potty until the day he died in nineteen ninety-two. According to Nick, I was potty in the literal sense of the word.

"You're crazy," he would say. "You are always doing things arse about face."

Until Dib mentioned it, I hadn't thought about a drink or going to the toilet. I was content just sitting in the back of the car, snuggled up under the car rug, all nice and warm.

"I would like a drink please," I said. The thought of a nice cup of tea was quite refreshing.

"Here's a place to stop," Dib said when she saw the lay-by. "We can get out and stretch our legs at the same time.

"Come on Potty," Nick said, helping me out of the car. "You can't stay there all day."

Considering it was January, the weather was rather pleasant, especially now that the sun was trying to get out.

"How far is it to Westcliffe?" I asked Nick inquisitively.

It's about twenty miles from here," Nick said thoughtfully. "I've got some business to do in Basildon first which will add a few miles to the journey."

"What have you got to go to Basildon for?" I asked.

"You mind your business," he said, dabbing the side of his nose with his forefinger.

I was surprised at how hungry I was. Sitting in the car, Nick unpacked the rest of the picnic basket Dib had prepared earlier. Each of us with cloth napkins on our laps tucked into chicken sandwiches, apple pie and had a mug of tea from the Thermos flask.

In contrast, Nick and Dib's way of life was so different from that of my Mum and Dad. Where Nick and Dib had no money worries and had the best of everything, Mum and Dad were struggling to make ends meet and had to budget their money accordingly. Here I was sitting in the car, eating good food and being treated like a princess. Whereas at home, even though we always had a dinner, invariably we had 'iffit' for tea.

"What's iffit?" Dib asked me one afternoon when we were having a chat.

"If it is in the cupboard, we can have it," I replied. "My favourite is bread and blackcurrant jam."

Gathering up the empty mugs, Nick said, "Do you want any more to eat Potty? There are some sandwiches left"

"No thank you." I said wiping my face with a damp cloth that Dib had given me. "I'm full up."

Before we set off for the remainder of our journey, we took a little walk in the adjoining field to stretch our legs.

Dib knew that I wanted to spend a penny badly.

"Pol," she said, pointing to a hedge by the far side of the field. If you want a pee, you'll have to go behind that hedge."

Making sure that nobody could see me, I arranged my clothes so that I could relieve myself. Unfortunately, I hadn't seen the stinging nettles immediately behind me.

"Ouch." I cried out when I stung my bottom

"Trust you," Dib said, when she realised what had happened. .

With my eyes filling with tears, Dib rubbed my bottom with a dock leaf. "That hurt," I said, embarrassed.

It didn't seem as if we had been in the car long when I saw a signpost marked Basildon.

"Are we there already?" I asked with a surprised look on my face.

"Yes," I heard Dib say. "You had a little sleep."

Once Nick had parked the car, it was decided that Dib and I would take a walk while Nick attended to his business.

"Come on Pol," Dib said. "Put your coat on and we'll have a look around the shops for a little while."

After about a quarter of an hour, I was complaining to Dib that my foot was sore. Taking a look at my foot, she said sympathetically: "Those boots you're wearing seem to be a bit tight. Did you bring any other shoes with you?"

"No, I replied. "Mum only packed my slippers."

"Never mind," she said. "We'll just have to get you another pair of shoes."

I couldn't believe it when Dib took me to the shop and bought me a pair of patent leather ankle strap shoes.

"Thanks Dib," I said exuberantly.

Going back to the car, we caught sight of Nick coming out of the jewellers shop.

"Is everything all right?" Dib asked, seeing the look of satisfaction on his face.

"Yes," he said. "Come on, we'll talk in the car."

Driving out of Basildon, Nick said. "It's only twelve miles to Southend. There's a prize for the first one who can see the sea."

Sitting in the back of the car, for what seemed like a long time, I was like the three wise monkeys. The conversation they were having was about the business that Nick was doing. Apparently, he was a silversmith and had a factory in Clerkenwell in London. The business that he had done in Basildon was taking orders for silver plated salvers and candelabra.

"What are salvers and candelabra?" I said, speaking my thoughts out loud.

"Earwig." Nick said, looking at me through the rear view mirror. "Don't be so nosey."

With that comment, I kept my mouth shut for the remainder of the journey.

"I can see the sea, "Dib said, pointing her finger. "Look."

Sure enough, as we were coming into Southend, you could see the gulls hovering waiting for their next bite to eat. I just wish that it had been me who saw the sea first although I never did find out what the prize was.

"It won't be long now before we're there," Dib said.

"Westcliff is only four miles down the road."

I was mesmerised, especially when we pulled up outside the large hotel. With big eyes I said: "I've never been anywhere before like this."

"Well, you have now," Dib said, before stepping through the double doors into the reception room.

After being booked in and shown the room where we were sleeping, I was so surprised that I couldn't talk. There was a double and single bed in the room and there was even a washbasin.

"Don't forget," Dib said. "If anyone asks, you are my daughter."

"Yes Dib," I managed to say, not really listening.

From what Nick and Dib told me later, if they had booked me in a separate room, it would have cost a lot more money.

"I didn't like you being in a room of your own," Nick said. "You're too young."

After unpacking our bags, Dib showed me where the adjoining bathroom was.

"Am I going to have a bath in that?" I said to Dib pointing to the big white bath with taps that ran hot water.

"Yes," she answered, putting some liquid in the bath that made the water smell nice. Before I knew it, I was undressed and was being washed in a proper bath. When I was finished, Nick dried me off with a big bath sheet, checking to make sure that I had washed behind my ears and between my legs. Dressed in my best frock that Dad had bought me for Christmas with clean white ankle socks and my new black patent leather shoes, I looked really nice. Dib had plaited my hair and tied it with a new satin bow.

"Are we ready ladies?" Nick said, once Dib had changed and applied some make-up. "Dinner will be served in a little while."

"We'll be ready in a minute," Dib said. "Why don't you go to the bar and get yourself a drink."

Ten minutes later we were shown to our table in the dining room.

"Thank you." Nick said.

Once we were comfortable, Nick spoke to the maître d' and then people began serving us food at our table.

"Why are we having dinner at tea time?" I asked Dib. "Why are we dressed in our Sunday clothes?"

As young as I was, Nick gave me the first taste of the way other people lived. It was during this meal that I had some lessons in etiquette.

"This is the correct way to hold your knife," Nick said, almost in a whisper.

I did as I was shown and as I tried to cut through my roast beef – whoops! The meat went one way and my vegetables went the other. The waiter, being a gentleman, never said a word when he mopped up the spilt gravy off the white laundered table cloth. I was so embarrassed. Fortunately, I never got any of the food over my new frock.

"Leave her be," Dib said quietly.

Dinner over, I was introduced to a lot of business people that Nick knew. They were all making a fuss of me, when one white haired gentleman said, "You look just like Margaret O'Brien."

Not knowing who Margaret O'Brien was, I just smiled at him and caught hold of Dib's hand.

"Who's Margaret O'Brien?" I asked.

"Shush."

"Let's go through to the lounge now," Nick said, looking at me. "We've got a surprise for you."

In the lounge, Nick had arranged a belated

Christmas party just for me. The Christmas tree was laden with presents, all with my name on it. I had a wonderful time. Come to that, so did everyone else.

"Potty, come here a minute please," Nick said, during the course of the evening. "Anne has lost a diamond out of her earring. Can you help us find it?"

Anne was another of the guests staying at the hotel and was getting quite flustered. From what I could gather, her husband George had bought her the diamond earrings for her birthday and wasn't too happy about what had happened.

I found the whole episode quite amusing. Anne's backside was the first thing I was introduced to. When I looked behind the chesterfields, she was on her hands and knees, crawling like a baby, searching for the lost diamond.

"I will help you look for it," I said, trying not to giggle. Off came my shoes and socks and treading the carpet, one step at a time, I began my search. Some of the other guests, especially those who had drunk too much, thought it was great fun and they began to look for the diamond as well.

"I don't give a fuck," a man said in a gruff voice. "Just find the bloody thing."

I pretended I hadn't heard. Eventually, I found the diamond, glistening, hidden in the pile of the carpet.

"She's good at finding things," Nick said, lying.

Exhausted, I sat curled up in one of the big armchairs, watching the antics of some of the people. It's surprised me to learn that whoever you are, whether you are from a working class family or born with a silver spoon in your mouth, you are no different underneath.

"Come on Pol," Dib said. "It's time you were in bed."

That night, I was so exhausted I was glad to get some sleep. Little did I realize that within twenty-four hours something else was going to happen to me that would stay in my memory for a very long time.

"Where are you going?" I asked Nick and Dib the following evening whilst we were sitting in the dining room, eating our meal.

"We have got some business to attend to," Nick said, abruptly. "We've arranged for you to go to the theatre."

"Who else is going?" I asked, quite concerned.

Dib's face broke out into a knowing smile and Nick answered saying, "You'll see."

After having a wash and changing into another frock, I was introduced to an elderly couple. I was told that they were going to look after me for the evening. I couldn't remember what there names were but the lady reminded me of Queen Mary. I wasn't too sure of her at first but after a little while realised that she was a kind lady.

The evening was magical. By the time the orchestra had tuned up, most of the people in the theatre had been shown to their seats. All the lights were turned off, with the exception of the stage lights and the show began. I was enthralled. When Billy Dainty came on the stage, he made me laugh. During the performance, he made a request for a little girl to accompany him on stage.

The gentleman sitting next to me gave me a friendly nudge with his elbow.

"Go on." he said, "Why don't you go up on stage."

What happened next was completely out of character for me but there I was being led up to the stage and Billy Dainty spoke to me. Looking at me with a twinkle in his eye, he said: "Are you ready?"

"Yes." I said, quite confident that I could do as he

asked. With the orchestra playing the music, I walked behind him, imitating his movements, singing the chorus: "I'm following my father's footsteps, yes. I'm following my dear old Dad."

With the applause still ringing in my ears, I wished at that moment that my Dad had been with me. We had all had a really nice time and I was sorry to say goodbye to the two people who had made my evening so special.

In the car the following day, on the way back home, I was still talking about the events of the previous evening.

"Dib," I said. "The lady even let me play with her necklace."

Slowly, winding our way back through Romford, I was unnaturally quiet, thinking about being home with Mum and Dad and wondering what we were going to have for tea that evening. Sensing my change of mood, Dib said, "Let's play I-spy."

CHAPTER 6

The School bell had rung. After assembly, all the children lined up and in crocodile fashion, made their way out of the hall to their respective classrooms. When my name was called out for the register to be marked, I did not answer. Where was I?

"Sandra Pink." Mrs Cox called out for the second time.

"She's not here Miss," Raymond called out from the back of the classroom.

Mrs Cox glanced over to the empty chair where I would have been sitting and with one movement of her hand, marked the register with a black circle, indicating that I was absent from school that morning.

In the staff room, during break time, Mrs Cox received a message from my mother that I had got measles and would not be attending school until I was better.

"Oh dear, I am sorry to hear that." Mrs Cox said when she heard.

Having only been at school for a few months, the last thing anyone expected was for me to be laid up in bed with a high temperature, not really knowing what time of day it was. My poor Mum sat by my bed for forty eight hours, attending to my every need before it was decided to send me to hospital.

Without further delay, the ambulance was called and I was rushed to hospital, wrapped in a large red blanket, with the sound of the ambulance bell ringing in my ears. A few days later, after the results of the tests had been received, the doctor contacted my mother. "Measles has turned to complications," he said. Not only does she have a highly contagious viral disease, she has pneumonia and nephritis as well."

Looking really worried, my mother asked: "What's nephritis?"

"Nephritis is inflammation of the kidney," the doctor replied looking very serious. "At the moment, she's very poorly and that is why we are not allowing any visitors apart from both you and your husband."

I was fast asleep when my parents came in later that evening to see me.

"I'm really worried about her Bert," said my mother anxiously. "She looks so pale and she has eaten hardly anything for over a week."

"At least she's in the best place," replied my dad, putting his arm affectionately around her shoulder.

Seeing the tears welling up in my mothers eyes, Dad passed her a crumpled handkerchief.

"It won't be too long before Sandra's up and about again. You'll see."

Sure enough, over the next few weeks, I responded to the treatment and there was an improvement every day. I was still terribly weak, but that didn't stop me clowning around. I had everybody in stitches with my antics.

"Sandra," the nurse on duty told me that evening, as we got settled down for the night. "Once the doctor has seen you in the morning, it looks as if you will be able to go home,"

"Do you mean it?" I replied, all excited. "Is my Mum going to bring my clothes in?"

"Yes. I have spoken to your parents and as far as I know, your Mum is going to come in tomorrow morning, after doctors rounds, with your clothes."

Once Nurse Hewlett was out of sight, I waited for a few seconds and not being able to contain myself any longer, I let out a shriek of delight. "Yippee!"

"I'll give you Yippee," Nurse Hewlett said, from behind me. "Now get into bed and stay there."

I knew from the tone of her voice that she was cross. As I climbed back into bed, it was more than I dare do, to look at the young girl in the next bed. If I had, we would have both had the giggles.

The following morning, Doctor Norton examined me and briefly looked at my notes. "Yes," he said, writing something on a sheet of paper. "You can go home today."

"When is my Mum coming to fetch me?" I said to the nurses whilst they were changing the sheets on my bed.

"Don't worry pet," said the nurse with a broad Scottish accent. "She will be here soon. You'll see."

I was not sure what to do, once my belongings had been taken from the bedside cabinet and placed into a white bag. Seeing my dilemma, one of the older children said, "Why don't you come and help us do a jigsaw? We could do with some help."

I was about to enter the day room, when I heard my mother's voice calling my name.

"My Mum's come for me now," I said. "I will come and say goodbye to you before I go."

"You're lucky to be going home today," said a little girl plaintively. "I wish I was going home too."

Once I had got dressed and said goodbye to everyone, I was eager to go home. Walking with my mother, making my way out of the hospital, through the winding corridors, I caught sight of a man in a khaki uniform, wearing a bush hat, waving at me.

"Mum," I said."Who's that man?"

"That's Uncle Clem," she replied. "Come on, I'll introduce you."

Uncle Clem was a very quiet man. He was painfully

thin but when he smiled, his whole face lit up.

"I've bought you a present," he said quietly, handing me a gift wrapped parcel.

"What is it?" I said mystified.

"Open it and you'll see," Mum said, laughing

I tore off the wrapping paper and couldn't wait to see inside the big white box.

"Let me help you," Uncle Clem said, taking the box from my arms.

Opening the box, there was a black doll inside, fully dressed with a red cape and hood. The doll even had shoes and socks on.

"She's beautiful," I said. "I am going to call her Little Red Riding Hood."

"I'm glad you like the doll," Uncle Clem said, smiling.

To hear Uncle Clem talk, you wouldn't have thought that he was born in Scotland.

"You've got ever such a funny accent." I said to him, indoors that evening, over supper.

"Don't be so rude," Mum said, disdainfully.

With everything that had happened to me over the last few weeks, I didn't realize how tired I would be when I got home. I felt quite feeble.

"Dad," I said, when I got up from the table. "My legs feel all wobbly."

Quite concerned, he felt my forehead to make sure I did not have a temperature. "I think it would be best if you go to bed early," he said. "Go on, get yourself into bed and your mother and I will be in to see you in a little while."

"Are you going to come in and say goodnight?" I said, looking at Uncle Clem.

"Yes," he replied. "I will tell you a story before you go to sleep, if you want me to?"

"Yes please," I said, rather too loudly. "I'd like that."

I remember saying goodnight to my parents and I remember Uncle Clem coming into my bedroom to read me a story but I couldn't tell you what the story was about.

"By the time I had read a few pages of the book, Sandra was fast asleep," he said.

It was late when I woke up the following morning. The sun was shining and when I looked out of the window, everybody was going about their business as if they had no time to spare.

"What's the time?" I asked my Mum, when I entered the living room. "It seems ever so late."

"It's nearly half past ten," she said. "You weren't looking too good when you went to bed last night, so I thought it best to let you sleep in this morning."

It seemed like a Saturday with Mum being home. Since I had started school, after the Easter holidays, Mum had got herself a little part-time job, around the corner. For the next few days though, with me being home, she had taken a few days off. Normally, she would have been in work by eight in the morning, when the factory hooter went off.

I was daydreaming when Mum spoke to me, whilst I was having breakfast that morning. A thought had crossed my mind to call my new doll Topsy instead. After all, Little Red Riding Hood did seem a very long name for her.

Looking directly at me, my mother said, "Sandra, I'm speaking to you."

"What?" I replied rudely.

"Don't say what, say pardon," she said severely. "How many more times have I got to tell you about that?"

Suitably chastised, I apologised for being rude and asked her when Uncle Clem was going to come and see us again.

"It is doubtful that we will see him again," she said, almost in a whisper.

"Why not," I asked. Where is he going?"

"You're always asking questions," she said. The trouble with you is that you want to know the ins and outs of a duck's arse."

"No I don't," I said indignantly.

Rather than cause her further discomfort, by me asking more questions at an inappropriate time, she decided to sit down with me and let me know all about Uncle Clem. She explained that he had been captured during the war and had been taken to a Japanese prison of war camp.

"Oh!' I said. I had heard dad talk about prisoners of war but I had no idea what a prison of war camp was like.

With a quiver in her voice, she said: "The Japanese were unkind to him. They were cruel. You have no idea what he went through."

During the conversation, she told me that as a child, Uncle Clem and Harry, his brother, had gone to live in New Zealand with other members of their family.

"I didn't know Uncle Keith had another brother," I said.

"Yes," she replied. "When the family split up, when they were children, Uncle Keith didn't go with them to New Zealand; he went into Dr Barnado's Children's Home and when he was old enough, joined the Royal Navy."

"Why didn't he go with them?" I asked inquisitively.

"I don't know," Mum answered. "I'm just telling you

what happened. All I know is that after the war, Clem wanted to visit his relatives in Scotland and from there, traced his brother, your Uncle Keith to England."

"Is he staying with Auntie Eileen and Uncle Keith at the moment?" I asked inquisitively.

"He was," she answered. "You've got to understand that until this visit, they hadn't seen each other for a very long time and they have a lot of catching up to do. From what your Auntie Eileen has told me, they are taking Clem to the airport this afternoon, to see him off."

"Where's he going?" I asked again.

"New Zealand. That is his home now. He does have a wife and family of his own you know."

I didn't say anything straight away.

"I would like to have seen Uncle Clem before he left." I said, almost as an afterthought.

"Time is getting on," Mum said, looking at the clock on the mantelpiece. "Come on, we'll have to get our skates on. "Your dad will be home in a minute for his lunch and I haven't done anything yet."

"Okay."

Not much was said about Uncle Clem after that and we never did see him again.

I liked Uncle Clem. He was so much different from his brother. Where Uncle Clem was a kind man and made me laugh, I felt very uncomfortable around Uncle Keith. To be honest, I was scared of him and when he looked at you, it felt as if his eyes bore straight through you. He was evil.

One thing that always did puzzle me though was 'who was Iris?' From what I remember as a child, some twelve months later, Iris, Uncle Keith's niece from New Zealand, came over to stay for a little while. We were about the same age and on the few occasions we did meet, we played together quite happily and had some photos taken of us together on our bikes. I thought no more about her visit until years later, when looking through some old photos that had been hidden away in a shoe box, I saw them.

"Look!" I said, studying the photographs. "You can't tell us apart. We look like identical twins."

"Must be a double exposure," was the reply.

The resemblance was uncanny. Was she Uncle Clem's daughter? I don't know. It's too late to ask questions now. Isn't it?"

CHAPTER 7

Nineteen fifty-three was the year the Queen was crowned. I was eight years of age and growing up fast. Everywhere, street parties were being held and it was a time of celebration.

"I am looking forward to the party," I said excitedly, whilst Nan was brushing my hair. "What time does it start?"

"Three o'clock," she answered. "Grace, my neighbour's little girl, will be arriving about half past two, so once you have both changed into your fancy dress costumes, you can walk down the road together."

Pop worked at the gasworks nearby and since being allocated accommodation that went with the job, had made a lot of new friends. All the people living in Kimberley Road, where my Nan and Pop now lived, had contributed in some way or another to make this day special for the children.

Plenty of food had been prepared to place on the trestle tables that were lined up from one end of the street to the other. Some of the dads, dressed up as clowns, were organising everything, right down to the last detail. Even my mother, who worked at Deeko in Garman Road, had arranged for the supply of paper tablecloths, plates and serviettes from the factory. The atmosphere was wonderful.

Looking out of the window, seeing Grace walk up the garden path with her mother, I couldn't help wondering what her fancy dress costume was like.

"Hello," I said, quite happily.

Seeing the expression on my face ten minutes later was a different story.

"It's not fair," I shouted, clenching my fists like a

spoilt brat. "It was my idea to go as a gypsy. Why has Grace got to dress up as a gypsy too?"

Hearing what was going on, Mum was beginning to lose her patience and said: "Now don't start."

When I get angry, my facial expression naturally changes, but I have a tendency to open my eyes really wide and have a certain look, that to some people is unnerving. I wanted to win first prize. In my eyes, Grace was stealing my thunder.

"Sandra. Put your eyes back in." Mum said, seeing the look on my face.

Instead of feeling angry with Grace, who was terribly shy, I should have felt sympathy. The poor girl, I found out later, had very few friends. Her religious background put off the children she did make friends with, which was sad. If you were invited to tea, a prayer was said at the table before eating and her father, if in a good mood, would expect the guest to read the Bible out loud after a meal. There was no smoking or drinking in the house and if he heard anyone swear or blaspheme, then you knew all about it. 'Holy Joe' the neighbours called him.

As it turned out, Grace and I compromised and enjoyed the rest of the afternoon. Having won joint first prize in the fancy dress parade, we both walked away with a beautiful needlework box, full of threads of all different colours. I had never tried my hand at needlework but after that day, was determined to get my mother to teach me how to sew. The lovely linen tablecloth and napkins we used when guests came for Sunday tea were embroidered by my mother and over the years, she did a lot of crocheting and knitting.

The only other coronation street party that I was invited to, a few weeks later, was not far from Baker Street, near Regents Park. Nick and Dib, as children, lived a few doors away from each other in the area and Aunt Emma, Dib's sister, still lived in the vicinity with her husband, Uncle Fred. Freddie Mills we called him.

Like a lot of these events, people had worked hard decorating the street with bunting. There was a big Union Jack. Red, white and blue flags had been put up and there were a lot of streamers and other paraphernalia that had been put on display. Somebody had even rigged up a sound system and music could be heard in the background. Everybody joined in the festivities and once the children had eaten, the adults arranged party games. As the evening wore on, the chairs and trestle tables were moved to the side of the road and there was dancing in the street. Some of the adults got quite merry and I can remember Aunt Emma, Freddie Mills and Dib's cousins being there too. Joan, Marie and Joyce were all enjoying themselves, but I have fond memories of Emma's youngest daughter Mickey, who got so tipsy, she insisted on sitting on the bonnet of Nick's car whilst he drove down the street. It wouldn't be allowed nowadays because of the danger, but from what I remember as a kid, it was all part of the fun. Nobody got hurt.

I loved being with Dib's family. They treated me as if I was one of their own and on the odd occasion when we went to see Dib's father, Pop Baker, he would make a big fuss of me and tell me stories of how things used to be. When it came to teatime, he would look over the top of his glasses and with his tummy rumbling and a twinkle in his eye, he would say.

"How would you like me to cook you a nice bit of fish for your tea?"

Who could refuse? To this day, whenever I smell fish frying in the house it reminds me of Pop Baker, walking round his kitchen, wearing a white butcher's apron with a tea towel thrown over his shoulder.

When he died some time later, he did not leave a lot of money but with the twenty pounds that Dib got as her inheritance, I understood why she went to the kitchen department in John Lewis and bought a pan especially for frying fish.

As young as I was, my mind was confused because I felt as if I was two separate people living two separate lives. I began to realise at this time that Nick was sexually abusing me. Subtly, over the years, he touched me at inappropriate times when no-body was about and showed me things that a girl of my age shouldn't even think about. Instead of my mother telling me where babies come from, Nick showed me. I was naïve and thought that what was happening to me, happened to other children as well.

Nick and Dib treated me like a princess. They gave me pocket money and took me to some wonderful places. I could have had anything I wanted. Looking back, I am sure that Dib and my parents were oblivious to what other things were going on and I knew I couldn't tell anyone. Nobody would have believed me, would they? I did try to tell Uncle Keith but was treated to more of the same, so over the years, learnt to keep my mouth shut.

"If I had told you, would you have believed me?"

You could more or less set the clock by the routine that my family had got into over the years. Apart from everything else, I wasn't very happy during the time that I attended St Pauls Church of England Primary School in Tottenham. There were times when I was bullied and teased mercilessly and after school, with my Mum and Nan now working full time, I was looked after by a child minder, Mrs Angel, until six in the evening, when my Mum finished work.

Mrs Angel was a kind lady who had a grown up son, Bert, who loved fishing. I remember how he would take off his wooden leg when he got home from work and would sit with me at the dining room table and make artificial flies to lure fish when he went fly fishing. Some of the dry flies he made looked ever so pretty. On one occasion, I thought I would help him but after getting a fish hook caught in my finger and getting blood everywhere, I gave up and just watched. Do you blame me?

During the long school holidays, except for the last week of July and the first week of August when I went camping with my parents, I would stay with Auntie Rose and Uncle Reg in a little village called Cogenhoe in Northampton with their daughter Stephanie. I had some lovely times there and got to know all the children who lived in 'The Piece' very well. In fact, I had more friends there than I ever did in Tottenham. Looking back, perhaps at that time, it was the only place that I could really be myself and feel safe. Nowhere else in the whole wide world, would I have been allowed to go out in the dead of night with some other people, just watching the owls hooting or seeing nocturnal creatures going about their business. It was a wonderful experience.

When I was at home with Mum and Dad, the weekends were more or less the same. Going to Saturday morning pictures with Linda, my friend, was something we both enjoyed especially now that we were in our St John's Ambulance Brigade uniforms.

"Look." Linda said excitedly, as we approached the cinema. "It's a Shirley Temple film."

"That's good," I said. "I like Shirley Temple."

Having been given free entrance tickets to the

cinema, we sat with a few other cadets in the back row. Wearing our uniforms with a starched collar and cuffs, we really felt as if we were somebody. The first aid room was at our disposal and acting a lot older than our years, we took responsibility of the first aid box, usually issuing plasters to young children. On the odd occasion, we did no more than supply a glass of water to someone feeling thirsty.

We were growing up fast and the next few years just rolled by. Linda and I remained friends and with the St John's Ambulance Brigade, we were on first aid duty at the Regal many times and saw lots of films. The first time I was in charge of our group, I was sitting in my usual seat, waiting for the film to start and said to Linda, "I hope something interesting happens today. I don't like it when we have nothing to do."

Linda had mischief in her eyes and looking round the auditorium said, "You can never tell. Do you think someone will cut their finger, or better still, break a leg?"

As if tempting fate, sure enough something did happen that day. A young boy came up to us and said, "Can you help me please. My brother is feeling poorly with tummy ache."

"Where is your brother?" Linda asked, getting up from her seat.

Pointing his finger, the young lad said, "He is sitting over there."

Somehow, we managed to get the little boy into the first aid room and after what was a brief examination and asking him a few questions. I looked at Linda and said confidently, "We will have to get him to hospital. He's got appendicitis."

"Are you sure?" said Linda, looking all worried.

I had only been reading a medical journal a few days

before and James, the little boy had got all the symptoms relating to this illness. Who was I to know any different?

Having made a decision, I was going to stick with my instincts and duly sent for an adult to confirm my diagnosis and to make the necessary telephone call to North Middlesex for an ambulance. Within ten minutes, after having a chat with the duty manager, the boy's parents were notified and not too long after that, we saw the ambulance men wrap up the little boy in a big red blanket and place him on a stretcher for admission to the hospital.

During all this time, Patrick, James' brother, had stood very quiet in the room and apart from answering questions, had said very little. When he saw his parents walking toward him in the foyer, the poor lad suddenly burst out crying. He literally ran as fast as he could and hugged his mother so tight, that he nearly knocked her over.

Gently wiping the tears from Patrick's eyes, his mother said: "Can you tell me what happened?"

"James had been taken to hospital. He had a tummy ache and some men took him away in an ambulance."

Patrick's father, looking very concerned, decided to find out exactly where they had taken James and what was wrong with him. Speaking to the young lady on the sweet counter, he said, "Excuse me. Can you tell me where the manager is please?

"Yes," she replied. "If you go to the top of the stairs, his office is the first door on the left. If you ring the bell, just ask for Mr Thompson."

"Thank you," Patrick's father answered, making his way to where the manager's office was.

Having done our duty, we were thanked by one of the staff and were asked to leave our names and addresses in case they wanted to contact us for some reason or another.

"Is there anything else we can do?" Linda asked hopefully.

"No," she said brusquely. "If I were you, I'd go and sit down for a little while and watch the end of the film.

We did manage to sit down for a few minutes.

"What happened?"

We were inundated with questions from the others, right up to the time we left the cinema. When we got home, we told Linda's dad the events of the morning. Quite concerned, he asked, "Did you find out what was wrong with the little boy?"

"No," we both said at the same time.

"Knowing you two, I bet the poor kid had nothing wrong with him," he said, looking slightly bemused. "It was probably indigestion."

Linda and I both looked at each other and for the first time, I began to wonder.

We didn't find out what happened to James until a few weeks later. Anne Watson, our unit leader, received a letter from Mr Spencer, James' father, thanking the St John's Ambulance Brigade for taking precautionary measures by calling the ambulance.

Did James have appendicitis? No. By all accounts, after a long wait at the hospital, James was seen by a doctor and after being prescribed medication for a bladder infection, his family were allowed to take him home. Apparently, he hadn't been feeling well for a few days with a poor appetite and feeling sick but on that Saturday morning, James insisted that he felt better, so his mother allowed him to go the cinema with Patrick and his friends.

The cadets always met up on a Friday evening and after the letter from James' father was read out to those of us present; Anne Watson said, "Both Sandra and Linda did their very best. Thank you." Looking directly at me, she continued. "Just remember that a lot of illnesses have similar symptoms so it's best not to assume anything."

CHAPTER 8

Time was getting on. It was nearly half past five and Pop and Auntie Eileen were still not home from the football match.

"They must be playing after time." Mum said whilst putting away the shopping that she had bought from Sainsbury's that afternoon.

Like most Saturday afternoons, Mum, Nan and I would go down the High Road to do the shopping, whilst Dad stayed quite happily at home, pottering about in the garden or seeing to his birds. It had been a few years now since Eileen and Charlie Drayton, the people who lived downstairs, moved to Potters Bar with their children Maureen and Keith and having the house all to ourselves, Dad had spent a lot of the time decorating and getting the garden established.

Only recently, my bedroom had been redecorated in a nice shade of lilac, with pretty pictures of ballerinas embossed on the wallpaper. Mum, knowing Linda's dad, who worked at the Beutility furniture factory in Edmonton had managed to get me a bedroom suite at a reduced price. I was thrilled, especially after sleeping in the front room for so long. Whilst we lived upstairs, I had my single bed placed in the corner of what was once a dining room. As well as having my own belongings in the room, there was a large dining room table and chairs, a sideboard and also the old 'Joanna' as Dad would call our piano.

I remember, when I was naughty and lost my temper, Mum would lock me in that room, but instead of it being a punishment, I was secretly pleased and would spend time just finding my way around the keyboard of the piano until I managed to pick out a tune that I knew. Dancing and listening to music was my escapism and what fun I had.

When Pop, my grandfather, heard me playing a tune on the piano, he arranged for me to have piano lessons. This I did for a little while but when the price of the lessons went up from half-a-crown to five shillings, my mum said,

"I can't afford that. You'll have to give it up. Five shillings is a lot of money."

It was a shame really because I did enjoy those lessons.

Once it was decided that we had no further use for the piano, Dad wasn't too sure how we were going to dispose of it. Speaking his thoughts out loud, he said. "Who would want an out of tune piano that had seen better days? The dustbin men certainly won't take it away and if you contact the council to collect it, I think they charge a fee."

"I'll ask around to see if anyone wants it," Mum said, casually.

"Can we have it? Pauline Hakim, a young girl, who lived opposite, asked when she heard.

"It all depends on what your mum and dad have to say," Mum replied.

"I know it will be all right," Pauline said with a grin. "When can we pick it up?"

"Come and get it whenever you like." Mum answered. "You will need some help shifting it though, because it's ever so heavy."

No sooner said than done, Pauline came back to the house later that day with her brother Joe and other members of her family.

"Can we take the piano now please?" Pauline asked, when Mum answered the front door.

"Of course you can," she said, looking at the group

of faces that had assembled on the doorstep. "Will you be able to manage?"

"Yes," came a crescendo of voices.

What happened next was like a Brian Rix farce. With sheer determination and the help of some ropes, they eventually managed to manoeuvre the piano down the stairs, along the hall and through the front door. Once out in the street, Mum realized we had an audience. From across the road, a familiar voice called out. "Do you want a hand?"

The last I saw of the piano was when it was being pushed by at least half a dozen people along the middle of Willoughby Lane. Cars were hooting, the drivers were shouting but it didn't make any difference.

"Not much further to go now," I heard someone call out.

About fifty yards down the road, on the opposite side, Pauline's younger sisters, all laughing and giggling, were waiting impatiently by their front door for the piano to be taken into their house. With them being a large family, I wondered who would be the first to tinkle the ivories.

I didn't see Dad standing behind me at first. All the same, he had been watching what was going on.

"Are you all right Bert," Mum asked.

"Yes, I'm fine. Now stop fussing."

Seeing the expression on his face, Mum could tell he was remembering the happy hours we had spent having a singsong around the piano whilst he played. I am sure at that moment, he was sorry to see it go. Dad was a good singer and when he'd had a drink, would often sing and yodel at the top of his voice.

On one occasion when we went to Auntie Rose for Christmas, not only had Dad had a few drinks but so had Uncle Reg and by the time they got back to 'The

Piece' they had entertained a lot of the village, singing Christmas carols. Had it been eight o'clock in the evening, it would have been pleasant and the villagers would have appreciated their ensemble. One o'clock in the morning, it was a different story, particularly now that there were at least four other people who had joined them in their revelry.

"Cis, what's that noise?" Auntie Rose said to my mum as they sat sipping sherry in the front room, waiting for Dad and Uncle Reg to come home.

"Shush!"

What they heard was a dustbin being knocked over and the sound of men's voices singing *'If I were a blackbird I'd whistle and sing.'*

All this time I was supposed to be asleep but after hearing all the commotion, I got up to look out the window to see what was going on. What I saw was hilarious. Never mind about grown men. Anybody watching would think they were little boys, the way they were carrying on.

"Bert, get in here now." I heard my mum shout as she opened the back door. "You ought to be ashamed of yourself."

"Reg," Auntie Rosie said. "If you think I'm sleeping in the same bed as you tonight, you're mistaken. You stink of beer."

What I heard next was shrieks of laughter coming from the two men. Their friends, who were coming in for coffee, never reached the back door. They had decided that it was in their best interest to head in the other direction. Hearing raised voices; I pulled the bedclothes over my head and eventually fell asleep. I never had a chance to ask my cousin, Stephanie, whether she had heard anything. By the morning, you can imagine, most of Cogenhoe were talking about it, including the local bobby.

There were times, when I was naughty; Mum would get exasperated with me, especially if I wanted my own way.

"Sandra, will you please do as you're told."

Things were going on in my life that I was not allowed to talk about, so I suppose for a child who had not yet entered puberty, it was a lot to deal with. Too much had happened too soon. No doubt I will tell you about that later. Meanwhile, I will tell you about an incident that happened whilst I was at primary school that shattered my world.

I remember Mrs Hollingsworth was acting deputy headmistress at the time. After having school dinner, we had gone out to the playground to let off steam. Like most children, we had boundless energy and there was always somebody getting into mischief of some sort or another. Never a day went by without Mrs Wilcox, the playground mistress, telling somebody off.

"Richard," she would call out. "Get down off that wall."

"Valerie," she shouted. "Stop tormenting the little ones."

If the twins, Michael and Tony, were in one of their playful moods, anything could happen and often did. I wasn't the only one to get them confused.

It was nearly half-past one when the bell rang for us to return to our classrooms. Having less than five minutes to prepare for our next lesson, I was in the cloakroom, chatting with some of the other children, when I got involved in an argument with Elaine Rookby, about a golliwog brooch of all things.

"If you collect golliwog tokens off any kind of Robertson's jam jars, and send them away, you can get a golliwog brooch," I told her

67

"Yes, I know. My mum got one for me and I put it on my blazer this morning but it's now gone. I'm sure someone must have taken it," Elaine said, looking at me accusingly.

"Don't look at me," I replied, with a tremble in my voice. "I haven't got it."

As the argument persisted and our voices got louder and louder, Mrs Wilcox, hearing the outburst, made a point of coming into the cloakroom to see what was going on, when she heard Elaine say venomously: "I know something you don't know."

"What's that?" I said, worrying that I was missing out on something.

"I know you're adopted," she said. "My mum told me."

With that statement Elaine was gone. Mrs Wilcox was standing beside me at the time and looking up for reassurance, with tears welling up in my eyes, I said. "That's not true. Is it?"

The poor woman didn't know what to say for a minute. After gathering her thoughts, she said quietly. "If I were you, I'd have a chat with your mum and dad when you get home."

All I know is that my legs had turned to jelly. I can't tell you how I felt. If what Elaine had said was true, then it meant I didn't have a mum and dad any more. All that had happened since the day I was born was a lie.

I never did ask my parents about the circumstances of my birth. Like an ostrich, with its head in the sand, I didn't really want to hear the answer. It had been a nice feeling being loved and wanted. Now all I felt was rejection.

Now that I was older and Mrs Angel no longer looked after me, I had been given the front door key to let myself indoors. Alone in the house, sometime later, going through some papers that were in the sideboard drawer, I came across the adoption certificate, which confirmed that what I heard was true. Feeling numb, I coldly read the words on the certificate over and over again until I had memorised every single detail. There were so many questions I wanted to ask. There was a lot I didn't understand.

Suddenly, I heard Dad's key in the lock. As he entered the room, he glanced over in my direction to see what I was doing and all I managed to say was, "Dad. What's this?" holding out the folded piece of paper that was in my hand.

"They are my pigeon papers," he said, not blinking an eye.

I quietly replaced the papers that I had been looking through and shut the sideboard drawer. How I managed to stay calm and not say anything, I don't know.

Making my excuses, I went somewhere where I could have a good cry and just be on my own. I was deeply hurt and had a lot of anger inside me. At eleven years of age, I turned from a pleasant little girl into a horrible spoiled child. I rebelled.

CHAPTER NINE

Going home from school, during the lunch break, was
something that I wanted to do. At the time, I thought it
was a good idea. I didn't like the school dinners much
anyway. Today, Mum had prepared all the dinner, so
when I got indoors, all I had to do was put a light to the
gas and re-heat the stew. By the time Dad came in from
work at half past twelve, I had made a pot of tea and
was serving up dinner. As we sat down to eat, I was
rather pleased when I heard Dad say, "The dinner looks
really nice Sandra."

"Thanks," I answered, curtly.

After we had eaten, putting his hand to my forehead,
he said. "You're looking a bit off colour today, my girl.
Are you all right?"

What could I say? I so much wanted to talk to him
about the certificate that I had found but didn't have
the nerve.

"I'm fine," I said, getting up from the table,
collecting the empty dishes.

When Mum came in from work, a short time later,
I quickly said goodbye

"See you later." I called out before closing the front
door.

My head was going round and round. How was I
going to bring up the subject? I read on the certificate
that my name at birth was Frances Eirowen. Who was
I really?

Never mind about school. For once, I had more
important things to do. Besides, with the nit nurse
coming to the school after dinner, I doubted very much
if anyone would notice if I arrived fifteen minutes late.

Sneaking back into the house, after Mum and Dad

had gone back to work; I removed the adoption papers from the sideboard drawer and made my way into the kitchen. Clearing everything off the kitchen table, I made sure that not even a crumb could be seen. Now was the time for my plan of action. In my mind, I was sure that if I placed the adoption papers in the middle of the table, my mother would see it as soon as she came home from work and challenge me about it. I would just have to make sure that I didn't arrive home before she did.

Returning back to school that afternoon, I gave my excuse why I was late and after seeing the nurse, went through to the main hall where we were having a talk about road safety. Before I realised, it was half past three and nearly time to go home.

"Don't forget your homework in the morning." Mr Johnson said as we grabbed our bags and hurried out of the classroom, heading for the school gates.

On my way home from school, I suddenly fancied something to eat. Passing the empty café, I peered through the dirty window and saw that the place had been stripped bare, with empty boxes and a broken chair discarded on the floor. I felt sad as only a few weeks before, the café had been full of activity and there would be half a dozen or more of my school friends queuing up, at the serving hatch, to get a crust of bread and dripping for a halfpenny. Now the place was shut and a 'For Sale' sign was displayed for everyone to see.

"If I was to give you bread and dripping for your tea, you wouldn't eat it," my mother said when she heard. "Why didn't you come home and have something to eat?"

Walking down Park Lane on my own, I suddenly became aware of everything around me. I crossed the

71

road and deliberately walked past the old cottage that was supposed to be haunted. Seeing Barbara, a young girl I knew, on her way home from Coleraine School, we spoke about the haunted house.

"I wonder what would happen if we walked up the garden path and knocked on the door." Barbara said, mischievously.

"Shall we go and see?" I answered bravely.

We were both apprehensive but our curiosity got the better of us. Cautiously, we opened the rickety garden gate and made our way up the long winding path. The garden was like a wilderness, overrun with all different colours. As you walked further into the thicket, you could see foxgloves, hollyhocks, delphiniums and flowers that I had never seen before.

"They say the old lady who lives here is a witch," I whispered to Barbara.

"Don't be silly," she said, looking at me with her big blue eyes.

Neither of us said another word. A moment later, we rapped the letterbox and hearing a slow muffled sound coming from within the house, we hurriedly made our way back down the path and ran.

Stopping to catch our breath, in the chemist doorway, we saw Ann King, the chemist's daughter, who had just come back from her piano lesson.

What have you two been up to?" she asked, seeing us both out of breath.

When we told her what we had done, she laughed and told us even more weird stories that she had heard about the two elderly ladies who were supposed to live there.

Looking at her watch, Barbara said, "I'm late. If I don't get home soon, my brother will wonder where I am."

Once again, I was alone with my thoughts. I didn't know what to do. How was I going to face my mother? I was beginning to wonder if I had done the right thing. I knew she wouldn't be home for at least another hour, so to pass the time I called into Mrs Wilmot's house, on the corner of Shelbourne Road, to see her son, Leslie. Mrs Wilmot took in sewing, to earn a few extra shillings and the pretty clothes she made, out of a few pieces of material, never failed to amaze me.

"Come in." she said when I knocked on the back door. "Leslie will be home in a minute."

Waiting for Leslie to come home, Mrs Wilmot gave me a drink of squash and I helped sort out her button box. I was fascinated. There were buttons of every shape, size and colour. I had never seen so many.

"Do you fancy a game of chess?" Leslie asked me, when he returned from the shop.

"Yes please," I replied, looking at the new chess set that he had been given for his birthday.

As neither of us could remember which square to put the white queen on when we set up the pieces, we gave up the idea of playing chess until we had seen Mr Johnson, our schoolmaster, who was teaching us the game after school hours. Instead, Leslie got out his Meccano set and we started to build a mechanical model of an aeroplane. It took him weeks to finish it.

Leslie, Ann King and I were good friends and we would spend a lot of time together. Ann was a natural when it came to playing the piano and I would often sit and listen whilst she practiced her scales. At twelve years of age, she was proficient enough to play to an audience anywhere, not just in school concerts.

I couldn't put off going home any longer and when I turned the corner, going into Willoughby Lane, I saw my dad standing at the front gate with Freckie, our little cairn terrier.

"Where have you been?" he said crossly.

"I've been to Leslie Wilmot's" I replied.

Looking at me with an icy stare, he said, "In future my girl, let your mother know if you're going anywhere after school. You know how she worries."

"Yes Dad, I said, as he followed me into the house.

As I walked into the kitchen, I didn't know what to expect. When I saw my mum setting the table for tea, I felt so nervous that I couldn't speak. What was she going to say to me?

"Sandra. Can you put that back where you got it from," was all she said, handing me the folded piece of paper.

For a minute, I just stood there with my mouth open. I expected a reaction, but not like this. I thought Mum would bring up the subject about my adoption during the evening but she never did. It wasn't until many years later that the subject came up, by which time; I'd done some investigations of my own.

CHAPTER TEN

On one occasion when I didn't come home on time, Mum had called the police and reported me as a missing person. From what I remember, it was a bright summer evening and after tea, I was allowed to go across the road to play with Christine Cooper, who lived on the top floor of the flats, opposite. Whilst Christine and I were playing on the veranda, we saw Sylvia, a school friend of mine, on the pavement below. Beckoning for us to go down, we met her at the bottom of the stairway and she asked us if we wanted to play gobs or five stones as they were sometimes called, in her back garden. We both looked at each other and thought it was a good idea.

"Shall we?" Christine asked.

"Yes." I replied. "Come on."

Unaware of the time, we continued playing for what seemed only a little while, when we heard a man's voice call our names. "Sandra. Christine."

"Who's that?" Christine said, getting up to have a look.

Opening the garden gate, leading onto Northumberland Park, we came face to face with two burly policemen. As neither Christine nor I had told our parents where we were going, you can get a picture of what happened next. We were both severely told off and weren't allowed to go out on our own for a long time after that. The policeman who spoke to us made us promise that, at all times, we had to let our parents know where we were going, who we were going with and what time we were expected home.

Since then, I have broken that promise ten times over. I decided very early on, that if I told my mother everything that went on, her hair would have turned white overnight.

"At least you tried your best," Mum said, when she heard that I had failed my eleven plus exam. "We can't ask for more than that."

I was not very pleased with myself. I felt as if I were a dimwit. Could I have done better? Yes, of course I could. At the time, I was concentrating on other things, unrelated to the lessons in the classroom. Linda Keen had passed her exams and was going to Tottenham High School and Sandra Collis, who lived next door to her, had a place in Tottenham Technical College. Feeling sorry for myself, I just sat and moped all evening. According to the letter Mum had received, I was going to St Katherine's Secondary Modern School for girls after the summer holidays. The name of the school sounds posh doesn't it, but I assure you, it wasn't.

"Bert," I overheard Mum say, when I was going to bed a few weeks later. "I don't know how we are going to afford to buy Sandra a school uniform."

"Don't worry," Dad replied. "I'll see about doing some overtime on Saturday mornings. "We'll manage somehow."

I knew things were difficult for my parents. For nine weeks when Dad was off sick with pneumonia, he never got a penny. My poor mother had got enough to cope with, working all hours to help pay the bills and put food in our bellies. Never mind about the worry when Dad was ill. At the time, I really didn't appreciate the situation. I resigned myself to the fact that I was going to St Katherine's and all I knew was that I wanted to be the same as the other girls. I wanted the best and wasn't prepared to compromise.

"Where do you think all the money is going to come

from?" Mum said, after I had given her a hard time. "Money doesn't grow on trees you know!"

As it turned out, Nan took me out one Saturday afternoon to Fred Wade's, the shop that supplied the uniforms and she rigged me out completely. It must have cost her a fortune.

"Nan," I said, when I tried on a blazer. "The sleeves are too long."

"Never mind, she said. "You'll have grown into it by next year."

What could I say!

By the time I started my new school, I had everything I wanted and more. Pop bought me a new leather satchel and Mum and Dad had got me a new pair of black sensible shoes. The only thing I didn't get was a brassiere or bra as they call them nowadays.

"No," Mum said, when I asked her if she would buy me one. "You are only eleven. There's plenty of time yet.

It didn't matter how much I argued, she was adamant.

Running about in the sports field, with my boobs bouncing up and down, I was not only embarrassed but was uncomfortably sore. When I spoke to Rosemary, my school friend about it, she said "If you go to Brampton's in the High Street, they have got some bras in the window for two shillings and eleven pence."

"I know what I'll do," I replied. "I'll buy myself one."

That is exactly what I did. Nick had given me half-a-crown for being a good girl and by the time Dad had given me two shillings pocket money that week, I had more than enough in my purse. I worked out that if I bought myself a bra, I would have enough money left over for some sweets and anything else that I wanted.

I couldn't wait.

When I went into Brampton's on Monday, after school, a female shop assistant served me. After putting a tape measure around my chest, she went through her stock and handed me my very first bra.

"Thank you." I said, looking sheepish.

Coming out of the shop with a small package under my arm, I felt pleased with myself and guilty at the same time. I was worried what my mum was going to say.

After tea, Linda came to the house and on the pretext of playing Lexicon, a card game in which you make up different words; we shut ourselves in the bedroom where I had shown her what I had bought.

"Pinky," she said, quite tickled that I was getting in a muddle trying them on. "Are you sure they are the right size?"

Hearing us laughing, Mum came into the bedroom to see what we were getting up to.

"What on earth," she managed to say, not finishing the sentence.

Seeing the predicament I was in, her face softened. "Come here," she said. "Let me do it."

For the next few minutes, Mum adjusted the straps and securely fastened the hooks and eyes at the back.

"Have a look at yourself in the mirror." Mum said.

If nothing else, it proved that the bra didn't fit me properly. Fortunately, Mum realized that I was growing up and on Saturday afternoon, she came with me to change the bra for one that gave me the support that I needed.

Growing up wasn't easy. It was far from it. Both my Mum and grandparents treated me like a small child and I hated being mollycoddled. I only had to sneeze and I was kept indoors, for fear of catching a cold.

Nobody could ever say that my parents ill-treated me. Not once did they ever smack me for being cheeky or naughty but there were times when I could scream.

"Children should be seen and not heard," I was told when I voiced my opinion.

Dad didn't really have anything to do with my upbringing. As far as he was concerned, I was his little girl who, like the nursery rhyme says, was made of sugar and spice and all things nice. If I was naughty, one look from Dad was all that was needed to reduce me to tears. My inside would turn to jelly and I would bite my lip, rather than let him see me cry. I can't remember him ever giving me a hug or a kiss but I adored him and have never forgiven myself for some of the nasty things that I said to him or my mother in anger.

There was always a mystery in our house, about what happened to the silver three-penny pieces. Well, after all this time, I will let you into a secret. I took them. I suppose in my own way, I was making a statement. After all, the money was mine, so why should I have to tell anyone how I spent it? I had no regard for the fact that up until 1950 when they stopped being legal tender, Nan, my grandmother, had saved the coins for me out of her housekeeping money.

During the school holidays, Linda and I would go swimming down the municipal baths but on this particular Saturday, for some reason or another, my mother refused to let me go.

"Why can't I go Mum?" I said, in a huff.

"Because I said so," she answered crossly as she was making her way up the stairs to make the beds.

In defiance, without my mother seeing me, I took the little white purse, which contained all the silver three-penny pieces, from the drawer in the sideboard and put them in a duffle bag with my swimming gear.

Going to the top of the stairs, I asked my mother again whether I could go swimming.

"I have told you once already," she said. "The answer is no."

Looking directly at her, I shouted, without remorse. "You're rotten."

"What did you say?"

From the look on my mother's face, she was shocked and hurt that I had spoken to her like that, but at the time, I felt completely numb towards her. Not wanting to hear what else she was about to say, I ran down the stairs, grabbed hold of my duffle bag, which I had left in the passage and ran out of the house, slamming the front door behind me. I continued running down Willoughby Lane and didn't stop until I had turned the corner, leading to Park Lane.

Because silver three-penny pieces were no longer in circulation, I knew that if I went to the bank, they were obliged to exchange them for the current value, which at that time amounted to over six shillings. Today, it is doubtful that a bank would let a child do any kind of transaction over the counter, without an adult being present, but in nineteen fifty-six I exchanged the money without any problem at all.

Meeting Linda, later that day, we did go swimming and thoroughly enjoyed ourselves. On the way home, with the change that I had in my pocket, we bought a packet of five Senior Service cigarettes and a box of matches from the newsagents. It wasn't the first time that I had put a lit cigarette to my lips but this time, egging each other on, we virtually made ourselves sick as we tried to mimic the grown ups.

"What shall we do now?" I said to Linda, not wanting to go home.

"Let's go back to my house," she said. "We can play

a game or something."

When we returned to Linda's house, her Mum and Dad had gone shopping and being bored and rebellious, we played the game 'Dare, Truth or Promise.' Some of the things we dared each other to do were usually quite tame but with a box of matches in our possession, we dared each other to strike a match, to see how long we could keep the flame alight, without it burning our fingers. Considering we were indoors at the time, it's a wonder we didn't burn the house down.

On the way home that afternoon, I knew that I was going to get a telling off but I wasn't particularly worried. I had done exactly what I wanted to do, so as far as I was concerned, what difference would it make.

"Where do you think you've been, young lady?" Dad asked when I eventually arrived home.

"I've been round Linda's house," I replied cheekily, only telling him part of the truth.

Seeing the impertinent look on my face, he proceeded to give me a lecture and gave me a severe telling off for speaking to my mother the way I did.

"Don't you ever speak to your mother like that again," he said. "Do you hear me?"

"Yes Dad." I said, biting my lip.

"I mean it," he said. "Now get that duffle bag of yours unpacked."

I don't know what came over me that day. Perhaps in my own way, I was crying out for help. Why hadn't they told me I was adopted? Why couldn't they see that I was hurting inside? Why did they always take things at face value? What was my secret? Crying my eyes out, upstairs on the landing, I looked through the banisters and yelled out in frustration. "You can't tell me off. You're not my dad, anyway."

CHAPTER ELEVEN

It was no shock to my mother when I came home from the hairdressers after having my hair cut really short.

"What do you think Dad? Do you like my new hair style?" I asked, doing a little twirl.

"It doesn't look too bad," Dad replied, looking up from his newspaper. "At least it's tidy."

You wouldn't believe that only a few years before, I had such long hair that even when it was plaited, it would reach down as far as my bum.

"You've got lovely hair Sandra." Mum would say when she brushed my hair in the evenings. "Wish I had hair as thick as yours."

Much to my dismay, I had no option but to have my hair cut. It was during the school holidays that my Nan took me and a friend to London zoo for the day and whilst we were in the children's corner, a nanny goat had chewed my pigtails.

"Ouch!" I said at the time, thinking Brenda, my friend, was teasing me. "Stop pulling my hair."

At first, nobody took any notice. The next minute, it seemed as if everyone was looking in my direction and laughing.

"Stop it," I said turning my head and seeing the nanny goat chomping at my plait. I was scared.

"Don't be frightened," Mr Graham, the zookeeper said, coming to my rescue. "Just stand perfectly still."

I did what I was told and fortunately, he enticed the goat away.

"It was the yellow ribbon in your hair that attracted her," he said quite concerned. "Are you all right?"

"Yes," I managed to say, almost in tears.

After all the fuss has died down, Nan tidied up my

hair the best she could and by the time we got home and the story was repeated to my mum and dad, even I ended up laughing, though I wasn't pleased at the time.

When I went back to school, after the holiday, with my hair professionally cut and styled, my friends at school thought I was joking when I told them what had happened.

"I don't believe you," said Rosemary.

"Well," said another. "I've never heard of a nanny goat chewing somebody's hair before."

"If you don't believe me, ask Brenda." I said indignantly, "She'll tell you what happened."

Whether they believed me or not, I was glad that my hair had been cut short. It was much easier to manage, especially now that I went swimming a lot.

"What do you call that hairstyle?" Christopher, a young lad at the swimming baths asked.

"It's called a DA." I answered. Trying to sound grown up, I whispered "It's an abbreviation of duck's arse."

"I've never heard that one before," he said with a grin.

I don't know who started laughing first but we both ended up with a fit of the giggles and we just couldn't stop.

Since going to an all girls' school, I was beginning to get more assertive and would argue if I didn't get my own way.

"I don't know where you get it from," my mother said, horrified when I answered her back. "Just you wait 'til your father gets home!"

I wanted to go out more with the older girls from school. Not just going for bicycle rides with Linda or going swimming at the municipal baths. I wanted to go dancing at 'The Royal' on a Saturday afternoon. I wanted to go roller-skating at Alexandra Palace. I wanted to do what the other girls in my class did.

"Mum," I said one Saturday evening, whilst we were in the front room, watching television. "Can I go to Ann's birthday party next Saturday?"

"You'll have to ask your father," she replied.

For once, my parents let me go, on the condition that I would be home before nine o'clock that evening.

"Thanks Mum," I said, looking forward to telling Ann that I could go.

What I didn't tell my mother was that some of the boys from the grammar school had been invited as well. As it turned out, I did go to the party and thoroughly enjoyed myself. Mind you, when I got home, I did tell my parents the truth and told them that we played postman's knock. From what my mother said, she didn't like the idea at all but what she didn't comprehend was that I was in less danger, mixing with a group of teenagers, than I was with a member of my own family.

The party was the topic of conversation on Monday, when I returned to school and before I knew it, another day was over.

"Come on Sandra," said Miss O'Brian, our sports mistress. "It's four o'clock and I want to go home, even if you don't."

"Yes Miss," I said realising the time.

I quickly grabbed my belongings and ran to the school gates, knowing that Nick and Dib would be waiting outside for me.

Since Nick had sold the silver plate factory in Clerkenwell, he had gone into partnership with his best friend Bert Brookes, a bookmaker. They appeared to be doing very well but sadly, when Bert died suddenly, Nick lost all interest in the business and decided to do something completely different.

"There's an antique shop in Palmers Green that I'm interested in." he said, speaking to Dib over the weekend. "As the shop premises have now become available, I have arranged with the vendor for us to view the property on Monday afternoon."

"Where is it?" Dib asked, thinking this was another of Nick's harebrained ideas.

"The shop is in Green Lanes, he answered."

Glancing over the top of his spectacles, he said, "Potty. Why don't you come along with us? It will be interesting to know what you think."

"Thanks," I replied. "I would like that.

"We don't have to be there until quarter to five and we can pick you up after school."

Dib and I looked at each other and knew that it wouldn't make any difference what we said. Nick would only do what he wanted to do anyway.

Out of courtesy, I did mention to my parents that Nick and Dib were taking me out after school but by this time, apart from sleeping, I was always at their house in Park Lane. Mum and Dad didn't seem to mind. Apart from which, they worked until 6 o'clock in the evenings and it meant that I didn't have to be left on my own. After all, I had known Dib all my life so what harm could I come to.

"Oh no," I said, out loud.

"What's the matter?" Dib said when I clambered over her to get in the Dormobile.

"I've just seen Uncle Keith," I exclaimed. "He is on the motorbike behind us."

"Where is he now?" Nick asked, seeing the worried expression on my face.

"Behind the black car," I answered in a tremulous voice.

85

As Nick pulled out to get in the main stream of traffic, he glanced in the mirror and saw Uncle Keith sitting astride his motorbike looking angry because I had completely ignored him.

"Are you all right Pol?" Dib asked after a little while"

"Yes," I replied. "I'm fine now."

It took us just over ten minutes to get to Palmers Green in the Dormobile and all the time, I was worried in case Uncle Keith had decided to follow us. I breathed a sigh of relief when we got to our destination and he was nowhere in sight.

At the end of the day, as all the finances were in order and Nick and Dib liked the property, they put in an offer.

"This calls for a drink," Nick said, as we made our way back to Tottenham.

"There's a bottle of wine in the fridge," Dib reminded him.

He looked at her in astonishment and said. "Never mind the wine. When we get home, I'll go over the off licence and get us a bottle of champagne.

As we turned the corner, making our way down Park Lane, I vaguely heard someone say something to me but I was in a world of my own.

"Penny for your thoughts," Dib said, seeing the blank expression on my face. "I know something is wrong."

"Averting my eyes, not wanting her to read my thoughts, I said calmly, "I'm okay."

"You know if anything is worrying you, we can always have a chat and perhaps I can help sort out whatever is the matter."

"I know." I replied, not wanting to talk.

"You look a little pale," she said, feeling my

forehead.

There wasn't much Dib didn't know. I had told her most things, including the embarrassment I felt, when I had my first period. What I hadn't told her was how unpleasant Keith was when there was nobody around. Nick knew. He was the only one I had told but whether he had said anything to Dib or not, I didn't know. I doubt it because if the truth be known, Nick had also been doing things to me from a very early age.

"Come on," Dib said. "Let's get you indoors."

It was the thought of seeing Uncle Keith at the school gates that afternoon that bought all the memories flooding back. What did he want? Was he going to follow me?"

I was only nine when I first told Nick what Keith had done to me. At that time, when I had told him, he wanted to know whether Keith was the one who had broken my hymen.

"What's a hymen?" I asked innocently, not having heard the word before.

He explained gently that when you are a virgin, your hymen is intact.

"When sexual intercourse takes place for the first time, the hymen, a membrane which partially closes the opening of the vagina, is broken," he said. "Has Keith penetrated you with his penis?"

"No," I answered honestly.

I did know what a penis was because we had discussed the subject of male genitals at St John's Ambulance Brigade. Not only that, I had seen Nicks. The only difference was that being youngsters, we had referred to the male sexual organ as a willy.

"He hurt me ever so much, when he pushed his fingers inside me," I said.

Nick was quite concerned and wanted to know

whether I wanted to blackmail him. I thought at the time that it was an unusual thing for him to say under the circumstances. There I was, discussing something that had really upset me and even though Nick appeared to have compassion for what had happened, he took the news rather differently from what I expected.

"Tell me exactly what happened, Pot," he said after a little while.

Sitting on the floor, with my knees tucked under my chin, I felt very uneasy but began to explain.

"All the family had gone to Auntie Eileen's and Uncle Keith's and after tea, Uncle Keith asked me whether I wanted to go up to the darkroom with him."

"Just take your time," Nick said, seeing how uncomfortable I was feeling.

"I knew that he was going to develop some photographs of Prince, their boxer puppy and I wanted to know what went on in the darkroom."

"Go on," Nick said, now very interested.

"We hadn't been in there long and I was fascinated, watching a photograph appear on a white piece of paper."

"What happened then?" Nick asked.

Getting more and more fidgety, I said. "I heard the sound of the ice cream van outside and Uncle Keith asked me if I wanted to get an ice cream and when I said yes, he told me to put my hand in his pocket to get out the money. When I did this, there was no lining in his pocket and he didn't have any underpants on. What I felt was his willy."

"The bastard." Nick said. "What did he do then?"

I explained how frightened I was and continuing the story, said. "When I told him I was going to tell my dad, he threatened me with his fist. I was too scared to tell someone after that and he pinned me to the wall and messed about with my clothes and pushed his fingers up inside me."

By the time I had told Nick all about it, I was crying and shaking with the thought of Uncle Keith touching me the way that he had.

Nick, seeing my distress, encouraged me to sit on his lap so that he could give me a cuddle. Curled up on his lap, with my head buried in his chest, I began to calm down as he gently stroked the back of my neck.

"He really hurt me Nick," I said. "He is a horrible man and he scares me.

"You're sure that he never put his penis inside you?" Nick said. "He never fucked you?"

"No Nick. Honest." I said, wondering why Nick had doubted my word.

This all happened a few years before but I can still remember Nick straightening himself up and saying, "Dib will be home in about fifteen minute. If I were you, I would go and wash your face before she comes in."

In the bathroom, I looked in the mirror and noticed that my eyes were all red and puffy where I had been crying. After I had washed my face and hands, I heard Nick call up the stairs. "Come on Potty," he said. "Grab your coat; we're going for a ride in the car."

"Where are we going?" I asked.

"I want to surprise Dib and buy her some flowers."

CHAPTER TWELVE

Over the next few weeks, everything I did seemed to be going wrong. I couldn't concentrate on anything and at school, because I had been cheeky and hadn't handed in my homework, I was given detention.

"Sandra Pink." Miss Walker, the geography teacher shouted, over the noise in the classroom. "I want you to stay after school and write one hundred lines."

Rudely, I ignored her and turned my back and spoke to Barbara, sitting at the desk behind me. The next thing I knew I was being escorted to the front of the classroom.

"For your rudeness and insolence," she said crossly, "I have no alternative but to give you six strokes with the ruler."

A deathly hush fell over the classroom as she spoke. Everybody had stopped working and apart from the rustle of papers and the noise of pens being laid down on the desks, nobody said a word.

"Hold your hands out, palms upwards," Miss Walker said, as she reached across the desk for the ruler. Feeling vulnerable, knowing that my protests would be ignored, I gingerly held my hands out and with an audience of the whole class, received six strokes of the ruler on each hand.

"If anyone so much as utters one word, you will all be put on detention." Miss Walker shouted angrily, addressing the classroom.

With my hands smarting and tears trickling down my cheeks, I returned to my seat. Nobody said a word. During the remainder of the lesson, the class was unnaturally quiet and not even the sound of a desk lid closing could be heard.

At the end of the day, when I returned home and Nan saw my swollen hands, I told her what had happened and she was ready to go down the school and see Miss Smith, the head mistress.

"Don't Nan, please," I begged. "It will only make matters worse."

Not understanding why Miss Walker had punished me in this manner, she began to ask me questions. "Why? What did you do?"

In Nan's eyes, I could do no wrong. To her, I was like any other thirteen year old who got into mischief sometimes. She didn't have any idea as to what was going on in my head or why I was so naughty at times. It would have broken her heart if she knew some of the things that happened to me. Things that I dare not speak about for fear of reprisals.

"I bet your Mum will have something to say when she gets in from work," she said. "If I don't go down the school, I bet she will."

What I didn't tell her was that in detention, I had literally drawn one hundred straight lines with the ruler. The teacher was not amused and as well as getting the ruler across my hand, I had to stay after school during the following week and write 'I must not be naughty in class' five hundred times.

Teachers wouldn't be allowed to hit students nowadays but when we were at school that was something that happened regularly. If we did something wrong, then we were punished for it. We fought, we argued and we laughed together and through it all, we learnt the fundamental things of life, which stood us in good stead for years to come. Yes, Barbara, Jackie, Rosemary and I have stayed in touch since our school days and as Jackie said recently, "Miss Smith would have been proud of us."

As far as the incident was concerned regarding detention, not much more was said about it and after a few weeks, everything was more or less back to normal. Yes, my hands were sore and so were Jackie Dodson's, who had also been whacked across the palm of her hand with the ruler for some unrelated misdemeanour but the pain was nothing compared to when I struck a firework match on Guy Fawkes Day. Linda and I had made a guy and much to our families' disapproval, stood on the corner of the street calling out repeatedly, "Penny for the guy. A penny for the guy! "

To our surprise, people coming home from work had thrown us more than a few pennies in the jam jar and feeling really pleased with ourselves; we went to the sweet shop in Park Lane and decided to buy some firework matches.

"Watch," I said to Linda as I took one of the matches out of the box. "These are better than sparklers. They've got a coloured flame that burns ever so bright."

Holding the open box in my left hand, I struck a match and before I knew it, the whole box of matches had ignited. Screaming in pain, my reaction was to let go of the box, which unfortunately landed on a rubber mat just inside the shop doorway. The smell of burning rubber was awful. I was upset enough as it was without the shopkeeper shouting at us. I was scared. Crying my eyes out, I ran out of the shop with Linda following just behind. We got as far as the corner and catching our breath outside Vic Aggas', the butcher's shop, who should see us but Nick as he was coming out of his front door. As he crossed the road to where we were standing, he shouted: What's the matter?"

"She has burnt her hand," Linda said, looking at me

sheepishly.

"Let me have a look," Nick said quietly.

"Ouch! It hurts." I cried out.

Everything happened so quickly after that. I could barely open my right hand it was so painful. I showed him what I had done and when I looked myself, I saw that all the skin on my hand was burnt and I could not separate my fingers. They had stuck together.

"Tell me exactly what happened," Nick said, looking very serious. "How did you do that?"

Sobbing now, I was unable to talk and Linda had to explain what happened. Without further ado, Nick told Linda to go home and I was taken into his house, where he put me across his knee and gave me a smacked bottom.

"That will teach you my girl," he said "You ought to have had more sense then to play with firework matches."

The shock of Nick giving my bottom a slap seemed to dull the pain in my hand and once my tears had subsided, Dib, who had been standing in the background whilst all this was going on, came and put her arms around me.

"It's all right," she said.

"Why was Nick so angry?" I asked as I heard the front door slam.

"Here you are," Dib said, handing me a clean white handkerchief. "Wipe your eyes whilst I go and find something to put on that burn of yours."

Gently, whilst wrapping up my hand with some bandage that she had in the house, she explained that because Nick thought a lot of me, he was upset that I had hurt myself.

"You'll have to understand," she said. "When he smacked you, he wasn't only cross with you. He was also relieved because he realised that things could've been a lot worse. Apart from which, he couldn't understand why the man sold you the firework matches in the first place."

"Where has Nick gone now?" I asked.

"He has gone over to see the man in the shop," she replied. "He won't be long."

Nick returned about ten minutes later and made his way to the kitchen where Dib had made a pot of tea. Straining my ears to listen, I overheard him say: "Bloody good job."

What Nick had said to the shopkeeper I don't know but from what I could make out, he was sorry that it was only the doormat that had been damaged. The way Nick was feeling, I'm sure if he'd had his way, he would have damaged the man's face.

"Come on Potty," Nick said, as I was finishing the cup of hot sweet tea that Dib had given me. "I'll walk you home."

When my Mum heard what had happened, I thought I was going to get another smacked bottom. I should have known better because Mum and Dad had never spanked me in their lives.

"Oh my God," Mum said when she saw the state of my hand. "I think we had better get you to hospital. Whatever were you thinking about, lighting firework matches in the shop?"

"I lit one to show Linda what they were like." I replied.

At the hospital, we had to wait an awful long time. Whilst sitting for over an hour waiting for the doctor, there were lots of people waiting to be seen with various injuries. Nurses were bustling about with no time to spare and men in white coats brought in a man on a stretcher, who had been in a car accident.

"Mum. My hand hurts," I whispered, trying to hold back the tears. "When will it be my turn to go in?"

"I'll go and find out what is going on," Mum said, getting impatient. "It's a good job I left your father a note, telling him where we are."

Making her way towards a curtained partition, trying to attract the attention of a nurse that was on duty, she pulled the curtain aside a few inches and the next thing I know, she had passed out on the floor.

"Mum," I called out, running over to where she was laying. "Mum!"

"Can someone get that lady a drink of water," I heard a man in a white coat say as he hurriedly went about his business. "We must keep that corridor clear."

Mum didn't like hospitals at the best of times and from what she told me afterwards, it seemed that when she took a peek behind the curtain, she had seen the burns of a little boy of about two years of age. Apparently, he had fallen into a bucket of nappies that his mother had been boiling on the stove a few minutes beforehand. Mum grimaced as she explained. "When the doctor removed the poor little boy's clothing, his skin had come away at the same time. It made me feel really bad."

It was something that my mother never forgot.

It was rather late by the time we got home and Dad was getting anxious.

"What happened," he said.

My mother explained all that he needed to know and ignoring the advice of the hospital, he took off the bandages, smothered my hand in Vaseline, and said, "There you are."

"Will I have a scar, Dad?" I asked, as he carefully put a white cotton sock over my hand like a mitten.

"No, I shouldn't think so," he replied, confidently.

It took about six weeks for my hand to get better and miraculously, I wasn't left with a scar. During that time I learnt to use my left hand for all manner of things. My handwriting wasn't very good though. It was more of a scrawl.

Sitting at home one afternoon, reading a magazine, an article explained that you could tell a person's character by their handwriting. Could that be really true? I wondered what conclusion they would come to if they studied mine. Especially now!

CHAPTER THIRTEEN

My parents were a bit apprehensive when Dib asked them if I could go on holiday abroad.

"You know she'll be all right with us," Dib said. "There's no need for you to worry about anything."

"What do you think Bert?" Mum said, anxiously.

"Don't look at me Cis!" Dad exclaimed. "Doesn't she have to have a passport or something if she goes abroad?"

"Yes," Dib answered "But that won't be a problem. If you can let me have her birth certificate, she can go on my passport."

"Cis," Dad said, as he took his cap off, scratching his forehead. "I suggest you go and put the kettle on and we can have a chat about this over a cup of tea."

A few minutes later, hearing what was being said, I entered the living room and with pleading eyes said, "Please Mum. Please let me go."

Dad gave me a knowing look and before Dib went home that evening; my parents had given their permission for Nick and Dib to take me on holiday with them.

I was so excited and kept asking all sorts of questions. "Where are we going Nick?" I asked when I saw him the following day. "Are we going to fly in an aeroplane?"

"No," he answered gently. "We are going on a ferry from Dover."

"Where is Dover?" I asked excitedly. "Is Dover a long way?"

"I'll go and get the map from the car and I'll show you," he said, knowing that I wouldn't be happy until all my questions had been answered.

"Here you are," Nick said, as he found the relevant page in the road atlas. "You can have a look yourself."

Map reading was double Dutch to me but with Nick's help I found out that Dover was in Kent.

"We worked out that it's about 80 miles from here, isn't it Nick?" Dib interrupted.

"Yes," he replied

"When are we going?" I asked Dib exuberantly.

"Soon," she replied, lighting up another Players cigarette.

"It's a pleasant journey though and you'll be able to see the white cliffs when we get there." Nick said, getting me even more interested in where we were going.

"Now be a good girl and get yourself off home." Dib said brusquely. "I'll have your mother after me if you're not home in time for your tea. Come on, off you go."

Dib helped me on with my coat and after saying goodbye, stood at the garden gate until I reached the corner of Park Lane. As always, I turned and waved to her.

"Bye," I called out, even though I knew she couldn't hear me. "Bye."

It had turned half past six by the time I let myself indoors. Dad had just got in from work and was out the back garden feeding the pigeons. There was no sign of Mum.

"Hello Dad," I called out as I made my way out the back door. He didn't hear me. "Dad," I called again. "Where's Mum?"

By the look on Dad's face, I realised he wasn't in a good mood. He never was when tea wasn't ready. Apart from that, he knew Nanny Edwards had been to the house that afternoon with the laundry. I never did find out why but over the last few years, he had hardly spoken a word to her. Whenever Nan came in one door, he went out the other.

"Where's Mum?" I asked again, hoping this time he would talk to me.

"Shush a minute," he said, looking up at the sky. "Shush."

I knew it was pointless trying to talk to him when he was in this frame of mind so I went indoors and put the kettle on to make a cup of tea. Wherever Mum was, she couldn't be too far away because her works overall and shopping bag were left in the kitchen.

"I've made a pot of tea." I said, as Dad walked through the back door. "Would you like me to pour you one?"

Before Dad had a chance to answer my question, I heard the key turn in the lock. It was Mum, looking really flustered.

"What's the matter?" I asked, quite concerned.

"Nothing for you to worry about," she answered, taking her coat off and laying it over the banisters.

Dad seemed indifferent. All he was concerned about was whether one of his prize pigeons that I had inadvertently let out of the loft would return home before it gets dark.

"Sandra, be a good girl and get a tin of corned beef out of the sideboard for me please."

Mum, still looking slightly bewildered as she started to set the table for tea said, "I've bought a fresh loaf of bread and there are some tomatoes in the fridge."

Whilst helping Mum with the sandwiches and slicing up some Madeira cake, I asked her why she was late home.

"I had an accident at work," she said, speaking very

quietly.

"What happened? I asked.

"A large sack of wax fell off the shelf at work and landed on my head," she said, rubbing her forehead. "I passed out."

From what Mum told me, the nurse was called from the first-aid room and Sid, her boss, had arranged for her to go and see Dr. Sterne, her own doctor soon afterwards because they were worried that she had concussion. Minnie, her friend from across the road, who also worked in the factory, had gone with her so that she wouldn't be on her own.

"Are you all right now?" I asked noticing how pale she looked.

"Yes, she answered. "I've got a nasty headache though."

"Take a couple of aspirins," I said firmly, convinced that Mum's headache would be gone within a very short time. "You'll feel a lot better then."

By the time Dad came back in from the garden to have his tea, Snowy, my Dad's prize pigeon had safely returned home and was securely shut in the pigeon loft.

"Thank goodness for that," Mum whispered to me whilst we were clearing up the tea things. "Your father would never have forgiven you if anything had happened to that bird."

Dad was a keen pigeon fancier and had kept pigeons since he was a small boy. He raced them and would sometimes go to race meetings with my grandfather, Pop Edwards. More than once, I had gone with them on a train with a wicker basket full of race pigeons and met up with other pigeon fanciers from all over the country. When released from the basket, one by one the birds would make their way back home and the winner was the first person whose pigeon was recorded to have made it home in the fastest time. Some racing pigeons are worth quite a lot of money and I have known Dad, when one of his prize birds laid an egg, keep it taped under his armpit until it was ready to hatch.

"Your father thinks more of those blasted birds than he does of me." Mum said, quite disgruntled.

In bed that night, I could not sleep. I was so restless, thinking all sorts of things. I was sorry for what had happened to Mum but mostly it was the excitement of going abroad that kept me awake. Nick and Dib had arranged everything and Dad had managed to get the old brown leather suitcase down from the loft in preparation for my journey.

"You're a bit short of knickers," Mum said, as she was packing the suitcase the following evening. "I'll have to get you some new ones before you go."

"Yes Mum," I said half-heartedly.

"I don't know where they disappear to," she continued. "It was only a few weeks ago that Nan got you some new ones from Marks and Spencer."

Feeling guilty, I made an excuse and hurriedly went to my room, supposedly to find a book. How could I tell her that I had purposely hidden some stained ones in my bedroom and that a pair had gone missing from the changing rooms when I went swimming at the municipal baths last week?

Before I knew it, the day had arrived for me to go on holiday. What I didn't know at the time was that in order for my name to be put on Dibs passport quickly, Nick and Dib had made a special journey to the passport office and waited patiently whilst everything was sorted out.

"Sandra, have you got everything?" Mum said, before we left the house to go to Nick and Dib's.

"Yes thank you," I replied.

Dad gave me an extra few pounds to put in my purse and made sure that the label, with my name and address on, was securely fixed to the suitcase. "Have a nice time," he said, as he made his way out of the front door to go to work. "Don't forget to send us a postcard."

CHAPTER FOURTEEN

Linda and I were growing up fast. We had been experimenting with make-up for a little while now and loved getting dressed up and flaunting ourselves, pretending to be grown ups. Now that we were teenagers, we wanted to grow up too fast. We thought it childish playing with children's toys. Why stay indoors playing the card game Lexicon when we can go window-shopping or go to Pymm's Park. Sometimes, when we had enough money, we would take a paddleboat out on the lake or meet our friends.

"You mind who you talk to," Linda's Mum said, when we told her where we were going. "There are some strange men in the park, who like talking to children, especially girls."

"Yes," I answered, giggling as we went out the door.

"Sandra, remember what I told you," she said. "If anyone comes up to you in the park and offers you sweets or anything, say no."

"Yes Mum," I answered.

"You go and tell the park keeper if any strange men want to talk to you or give you anything."

I acknowledged what she was saying and promised to be home before tea. Mum was worried about us going to the boating lake and the last words she said to us before we went were, "Remember, come straight home. Do you hear me?"

"Why do parents always have to spoil our fun?" I said to Linda on the way to the bus stop. Being facetious, I mimicked what my mother had said and continuing the conversation, said to Linda looking quite serious, "We have to talk to strangers when we ask for a bus ticket on the bus and we can't possibly walk straight home because we have to turn corners."

We both looked at each other and laughed. Counting our money, we decided that after having a go on the paddle boat and buying an ice cream, we would have enough money left for five Senior Service cigarettes and a box of matches.

"Where did you get all that money from?" Linda asked me, knowing that I only got half-a-crown pocket money on Saturday morning.

"Nick gave me some money when I went to work for him yesterday to collect some silver candelabra," I answered

"You are lucky," Linda said enviously. "I have to do jobs around the house to earn my pocket money."

What I didn't tell Linda was that Nick slipped me an extra few shillings because I was pleasant to him and he was teaching me things that only grown ups do.

"This is our little secret," Nick said, when he was pleased with me.

Linda and I enjoyed ourselves when we went out together weekends but our parents got anxious when we asked them if we could go dancing.

"You're too young," Dad said, when I mentioned it to him.

Speaking to Linda that evening when I went to her house to play Monopoly, I said, "It's not fair. We are too young to do the things we want to do and yet, according to the park keeper, we're too old to go on the swings in the play area."

Overhearing our conversation, Linda's father looked over the top of the newspaper that he was reading and said. "You'll grow old soon enough. It's no good wishing your life away."

"Mum," I protested, when I got home. "Why can't

I go to the 'Royal' dancing?"

"You're too young to be walking down the High Road that time of night on your own.

"Pearl and Nola are in my class at school and their mothers let them go," I argued.

"I don't care what you say," she said. "You're not going. Besides, you don't know what kind of people you'll meet in there."

I was quiet for a little while, my mind working ten to the dozen. Determined as I was to go dancing, I compromised and said, "Well, if Linda's Mum lets her go, will you let me go to the Municipal Hall on Saturday afternoon? They have dances there every week and it's only sixpence to get in."

"Well see," she answered.

Keeping my fingers crossed, I said, "Please Mum. It is for teenagers and some of my friends at school go. They are younger than me. Please Mum. Can I go?"

"I said, we'll see," she replied, looking at me sternly.

Saturday afternoon came and yes, Linda and I had persuaded our parents to let us go dancing. Setting off to catch a bus to Bruce Grove, we were in high spirits.

"You come straight home," Mum said when she saw us across the road.

"Don't worry about us Mum," I said rather off-hand. "We'll be all right."

Unbeknown to my parents, I had taken one of Mum's compacts and some red lipstick out of her dressing table drawer and put it in my bag.

"If my Dad saw me now, he would kill me," Linda said after applying some lipstick and powder. "You will help me clean it off afterwards, wont you?"

"Yes, yes," I answered, eager to get going. "Stop worrying."

"It makes a change from catching the 233 bus to Alexandra Palace, doesn't it?" Linda said when we eventually got a seat on the bus.

"Yes," I agreed. "I'm still going to go roller skating though. Mum and Dad are going to buy me a new pair of skating boots for my birthday."

"You've told me that already," she said, fooling around.

"It's all right for you," I teased. "You've already got a pair."

"Only because they were my cousins," she answered. "My aunt in Norfolk gave them to me when Marjorie, my cousin, died."

Not knowing what to expect when we arrived at the dance hall, we were pleasantly surprised. I was fascinated by the sound of the big band. To be honest, I didn't know at that time whether I fell in love with the music or the band leader, who was a gentleman in his forties with brown hair, a moustache and the most wonderful smile.

"What's your name?" he said to me a few weeks later when I entered a singing contest.

"Sandra," I replied, my face reddening.

I'll never forget that day. A lot of my school friends were there taunting me but as embarrassed as I felt, I sang the song 'Ma He's Making Eyes at Me' and received a free ticket to get into the dance hall the following week.

"Mum," I called out as I let myself indoors. "I won! I won!"

"Calm down." Dad said, wondering what all the noise was about.

Of course they were both pleased for me but Dad teasingly said. "You're no Shani Wallace you know. If you won the singing contest, what were the others like?"

Not knowing what to say, I said nothing but over the weeks, there were more than two occasions when they let me in the Municipal Hall free of charge.

"Have you got anything planned for tomorrow night?" Linda asked me when I saw her the following week.

"No. Why?" I asked, wondering what she had in mind.

"Dad said that if it's a nice evening, he would take us out."

My curiosity got the better of me and I asked, "Where are we going?"

"He did say that he would take us out in the country and buy us a drink," she replied.

Being cautious, I asked, "Who else is going,"

"Only my Mum," she answered. "He did say that you could come as well."

True to his word, the following evening, we all set off in her Dad's three wheeled mini car, including Bonny the dog. It was a bit of a squeeze but we managed. We stopped at a little country pub that was some way out in the country and both Linda and I were pleased to sit in the garden, playing with the dog and drinking a glass of shandy that her Mum had bought out for us.

"Do you want a packet of crisps?" her Mum asked.

"Yes please," we said, enjoying ourselves.

Linda and I often got together and whispered secrets to each other but this evening, whether it was the relaxed atmosphere, sitting quietly with the sun setting, or whether it was the second glass of shandy that I had drunk, I don't know. I just wanted to talk.

"Linda," I said quietly. "If someone you knew tapped you on the shoulder, handed you a wad of pound notes and said, 'Quickly, put these down your knickers,' what would you do?"

"I'm not really sure," she answered, looking at me with her big brown eyes. "Why?"

Just as I was about to tell her what happened, her Mum and Dad came out of the pub to join us and suggested that we went for a walk with the dog.

I'll tell you later," I whispered.

CHAPTER FIFTEEN

Talking in the classroom with my school friends, we were discussing the play Midsummer Nights Dream that Miss Abbott, our school teacher, had told us we were going to perform in front of the whole school at end of term.

"I don't know anything about Shakespeare," I said, quite perplexed. "I know he wrote a lot of plays including Twelfth Night and Midsummer Nights Dream but that's about all."

"What part are you playing?" Jackie asked

"I've been given the part of Puck." I replied. "I've seen the script but I'm never going to remember the lines."

"I'm playing a wall" said Sylvia, laughing. "When I'm on stage, I don't have to say anything but have to keep my arms outstretched the whole time."

"Are you serious?" Jackie said, with a twinkle in her eye. "I can't see that happening."

"You've got a part too, haven't you Jackie?" Sylvia asked.

"Yes. I'm playing Quince 'The Prologue."

Over the next few weeks, all else was forgotten. For me, I was so pleased to get a part and we were completely absorbed in learning our lines. All we knew was that our parents had bought tickets to see the play and we wanted them to be proud of us.

"How now, spirit!" I said, beginning to read my lines.

"Bottoms up," came a loud voice from the wings.

That was it, the beginning of the end for us. We had worked so hard to get everything organised and now, with all eyes on the stage for our one and only performance, we completely lost it. Someone fell over their shoe laces; Jackie was distracted and had to ad-lib because she had forgotten her lines and in full view of the audience, when Helena turned to speak, her dress at the back was caught in her knickers. Even the stage lights kept flickering. Not only were we in fits of laughter, but the audience were enjoying themselves too.

"Shakespeare meant this to be a fantasy, not a hysterical comedy." Miss Smee, one of our school teachers, said, before the epilogue.

"Yes miss," we said in unison, trying hard to stifle our giggles.

At the end of the performance, we were met with loud applause and cheering.

"Midsummer Nights Dream will never be the same again." Miss Abbott said, amused. There was some general banter and even the teachers in the audience were clapping.

"That was sacrilege!" Miss Smee exclaimed crossly. "Why didn't they follow the script?"

"The audience thought it was all part of the play." Miss Walker, the geography teacher, said, in our defence. "Under the circumstances, I think they did very well."

Travelling home on the bus that evening with Barbara and Jennifer, I glanced out of the window hoping to catch sight of where Big Nan used to live.

"There it is," I said out loud, pointing my finger toward a row of terrace houses. "Look! There it is."

"Where are you pointing?" Barbara asked.

"Never mind, we've gone past it now." I said, turning my head to the seat behind where my friends were sitting.

The bus continued its journey and I sat quietly on

my own thinking of the happy times that I had spent in the house. What happened to Uncle George and Dorothy after Big Nan died? Where was Dorothy now?

When Dorothy, my mother's cousin, married a foreign gentleman by the name of Zuebek Weltika, Laurie we called him, they rented a couple of rooms upstairs in Big Nan's house. Uncle George, Dorothy's father, also had a room on the same landing and the modest rent they paid, helped Big Nan out financially. Not only that but as Ardy, Big Nan's husband, was working abroad for most of the time, she felt content knowing there was always someone in the house. For a while, it was a good arrangement. Uncle George helped out with the decorating jobs that needed doing but apart from that, kept himself very much to himself. He was an avid reader and most of the time, spent his evenings alone upstairs in his room. Things started to get a bit overcrowded when Dorothy had a little girl, Genina, but it wasn't until she had another baby Monica, that there was talk of them finding a bigger place to live.

"We've decided to leave England," she told Big Nan and her father, one evening after they had eaten a hearty meal. "Laurie and I are going to make a fresh start in Canada with the children."

"That's a big decision to make." George said. "Are you sure that's what you want to do?"

"Yes," she answered.

For some political reason, which I didn't understand at the time, Canada was chosen because as far as Laurie was concerned, it was a neutral country. I always thought Laurie was Polish but apparently he was born in Yugoslavia. Something to do with Tito and communism I was told. All I knew was that he couldn't return to the place of his birth. He was not even able to visit to see his elderly mother when she was ill. Once Dorothy and Laurie had made their decision, they saved every penny they could. Every pay day, more pound notes were placed in the Welsh dresser and when they had accumulated enough money and all the arrangements had been made, they were gone. I never had a chance to say goodbye. I was really upset, especially after I heard that not long after they arrived in Canada, Laurie packed his bags, leaving Dorothy alone in a strange country with the two children and no money.

"Mum. What happened to Dorothy?" I asked, some years later, when someone I saw on television, reminded me of her.

"Oh, I don't know," she replied.

"Have you got her address?" I asked. "Only I would like to write to her."

"I've got it written down somewhere but don't ask me where it is now," Mum said, whilst she was scraping some new potatoes, ready for dinner. "Wonderland Avenue, Ontario is all that I can remember but she has probably moved by now."

Continuing the conversation, Mum told me that on one occasion, when Aunt Cis, Dorothy's mother, was doing some baking, she made Dorothy a bread pudding and knowing that her friends were flying out to Ontario the following day, asked them if they would deliver it to her.

"Did she get it all right?" I asked, imagining the look on Dorothy's face when a stranger knocked on her door with some bread pudding that her Mum had made in England.

"I expect so." She answered.

"How old is Genina and Monica now?" I asked inquisitively.

"I can't remember." Mum replied. "All I know is that in spite of everything, Dorothy struggled to bring up those two kids on her own and after getting a job, met some chap where she worked and he asked her to marry him."

"She's remarried then."

"Oh yes," Mum said. "From what Aunt Cis told me, Dorothy's husband thinks the world of her and the two girls. The last I heard, they had settled in Ontario and had a little boy. Ted I think his name is."

It's strange how you remember things as if they were yesterday. Alone with my thoughts, I can still recall helping Dorothy bath the baby.

"I haven't given her a name yet," she said, gently wrapping the little girl in a big bath towel. "Have you got any ideas about girls' names?"

After going through various names, I said. "I like the name Monica. You know, like that programme on the radio when someone says, 'What's your name?' and Beryl Reid replies, 'My name's Monica'."

Thoughtfully, Dorothy said, "I know the programme you mean. I like that name. Yes. We'll call her Monica. The name suits her."

Secretly, I was pleased.

After being at work in the gasworks all day, there was nothing Pop liked better than pottering about on the land and showing off his prize dahlias, which he grew from seed. Before he had the allotment in Willoughby Lane, he grew all the vegetables for the family on a piece of ground at the back of Big Nan's house.

There was always plenty of activity in the house and when Ardy retired and returned from India, where he had been working as a bricklayer, all the family were invited to tea to celebrate his homecoming.

"Hello Ardy," Mum said, as she went over and gave her grandfather a big hug.

"Nice to see you gal," he replied, giving her arm a squeeze.

Not having seen Ardy for a long time, I was painfully shy and after all the introductions had been made, and the grown ups had made themselves comfortable in the front room, I made my way into the kitchen where Nan was making cakes.

"Nan," I said quietly, seeing her busily measuring out the ingredients for a large fruitcake. "Can I help you?"

"Yes," she replied. "You can give this a stir if you want to."

Passing over the big earthenware mixing bowl and a wooden spoon, she proceeded to add the egg and the caster sugar for me and I mixed all the ingredients together until my wrist ached.

"I'll just grease and flour these loaf tins," she said. "Once all the mixture has been put in the tins, ready for the oven, you can wash these things up for me, if you still want to help."

"Nan, can I lick the bowl clean first?" I asked.

"You're as bad as your mother," she said grinning. "Cissie always licked the bowl clean when she was a little girl."

"Ginnie," Big Nan called from the front room. "Come and have a drink. You deserve it after all the work you've done in the kitchen."

I looked at Nan and said, "Why does Big Nan call you Ginnie?

"As a child," she said, "I couldn't pronounce my Christian name properly and when people asked me what my name was, instead of saying Elizabeth Jane, I said something that sounded like Ginnie."

"Oh!" I exclaimed.

Before I had a chance to ask any more questions, Uncle George came in from the garden. Taking his hat off as he entered the back door, he said in a refined voice. "Hello young lady, you must be Sandra, Cissie's girl."

"Yes," I answered politely.

"Pleased to meet you," he said, extending his arm, ready to shake my hand. We shook hands and he said, "I didn't recognise you in your new clothes."

Uncle George was a gentle quiet man, with impeccable manners but what I liked about him was that he made me laugh.

Big Nan, hearing Uncle George's voice, called out. "George, come and show your face."

For a brief moment, I thought I saw his expression change and after removing his jacket, Nan whispered to him. "If I were you, I would go and join the others. They won't be too pleased with you if you don't."

As we followed Uncle George into the front room, Nan looked at her husband and said, "You can pour me that drink now, Harold."

"What do you fancy love," he replied affectionately.

"Make it a large Gin and Tonic please."

Big Nan had about twelve of us for tea that day and we had a wonderful time. When the table was laid up, nobody moved until Ardy rose from his armchair and took pride of place sitting at the head of the table, making himself comfortable on the big wooden carver – an ornate dining chair that had arms.

Showing me to my seat, Shirley, Dorothy's sister said, "Here you are Sandra; I've set you a place next to Ardy."

"Thank you," I replied, remembering my manners.

Tea that afternoon was scrumptious. The table was

laden with all kinds of lovely food. We had red salmon sandwiches, tinned fruit with bread and butter and as much cake as you could eat. Because the family hadn't seen each other for a long time, the conversation over tea was varied. At one stage it seemed as if everyone was talking at the same time, but when Ardy started talking about India, nothing could be heard except the sound of his voice. He made India sound magical.

"Perhaps one day Sandra, you will be able to see those things for yourself," he said.

Bringing me back down to earth, Nan gave me a paper serviette to wipe the cake crumbs off the corner of my mouth and said, "Did you enjoy your tea?"

"Yes," I said, still thinking about the wonderful stories that Ardy has been telling us about India.

It was explained to me that Uncle George was married to Aunt Cis, Pop's sister but he hadn't lived with her for a number of years.

"Aunt Cis left him some twenty years ago and set up home with another man." Mum said, almost in a whisper. Ted I think his name was."

"Yes," I overheard Big Nan say. "George has never got over it. Cissie and Ted wanted to get married but George would never agree to a divorce."

Having seen Auntie Cis a few weeks before, I couldn't imagine her still being married to Uncle George. I had only seen her a few times, but what little I did know of her, she was a warm homely lady and was happy living with the man whom I thought was her husband and their two children.

Whilst the tea things were being cleared away, Pop said, "Would anyone like to go for a walk? I could do with stretching my legs."

"Yes, I'll come with you," Ardy replied. "Before it gets too dark, I'd like you to show me those prize

Dahlias that you told me about."

Not wanting to miss out on anything, I said, "Can I come as well?"

"Only if you put your coat on," Pop said, lacing up his boots.

Before going through the garden gate at the back of the house, Ardy stopped at one of the outbuildings to check on the barn owl that was kept there. Satisfied that everything was all right, we made our way through the maze of dirt tracks until we came to the plot of land that Pop had rented from one of the neighbours.

"Like you said Harold, these Dahlias will win prizes." Ardy said. "Those Chrysanthemums are coming on nicely as well."

They continued talking about different plants that I had never heard of and before we walked back to the house, Pop gathered up a nice bunch of flowers for Big Nan to put in the parlour. Little did I know that the next time I went into that room, I would see flowers laid on Ardy's coffin, waiting for the hearse to arrive.

For the short time that I knew Ardy, I liked him. He may have been a man of small stature with white hair and a white moustache that used to tickle my cheek when he kissed me but he had a big heart and was fun to be around. I remember once, watching him shave in the kitchen. Getting too close whilst he was lathering his face, he teasingly dabbed soap all over my chin and with an open razor in his hand, which he had sharpened on a strap hanging on the pantry door, he laughed and said,

"Would you like a shave as well?"

I ran.

"Come on Pinky," Jennifer said, thumping me on the shoulder.

"Stop daydreaming. We get off the next stop."

"Northumberland Park," called the conductor as the bus juddered to a halt.

CHAPTER SIXTEEN

Seeing Nick and Dib coming out of their back gate, I didn't know what to say. Why is it when you want to avoid someone, they always appear?

"How are you Potty?" Nick said, as I walked by.

"I'm O.K.," I said, gently stroking my right earlobe, so that he would notice. No, I hadn't had my ears pierced or anything like that. It was a gesture to let Nick know that I had started my period.

"That's all right then," he said, relief spreading over his face. "Are you going to come in for a little while?"

Looking at my watch to see what the time was, I lied, saying "No. I'd better not. Mum is expecting me home in a minute."

From the way Dib looked at me, I knew she wanted to tell me something but all she said was, "Nick is going to the city tomorrow. If you're not going anywhere, why don't you pop in and keep me company for a little while?"

Not really sure of what to say, I averted my eyes away from Nick and said, "Thanks Dib."

"I tell you what," she said. "Why don't you come over for lunch?"

"I will have to ask Mum first," I replied, thinking of the lovely salmon and watercress sandwiches that Dib sometimes made.

"I'm sure Cis won't mind," she said with a smile spreading across her face.

Unfortunately, my mother did mind. The following day, after Saturday morning pictures, I told my mother that I had been invited to Dib's and her reply was, "I'm surprised you don't take your bed over there."

It was getting increasingly difficult for me. Not only

did it seem that I was living two separate lives, I felt at times as though I was two separate people. At home, I was Sandra with working class parents who thought a lot of me. At Nick and Dib's, I was Potty or Polly 'Opkins as Dib sometimes called me. Dib was like a second Mum to me but with Nick, it was different. On our own, he treated me as a person, accepting my idiosyncrasies and said,

"Potty, if anyone loves you half as much as I love you, then they love you."

Almost in a whisper, I replied, "Yes, Nick."

"I mean it." He said in his loud booming voice.

If anyone else was present, he still treated me as an individual but played the role of a father figure, which was a joke in itself.

Not only was Nick teaching me about antiques, hallmarks and fine arts but he was also teaching me the facts of life in the literal sense of the word.

"As far as we are concerned, you are like the daughter we never had." Dib told me on one occasion when we were having a chat. "You see, we couldn't have any children of our own."

I didn't ask too many questions at that time, but now, I was beginning to wonder.

"Linda," I said, when the subject of infertility came up in one of our discussions at St John's Ambulance Brigade. "If Nick and Dib can't have any children, does that mean that Nick can still father a child?"

"Yes, I suppose so," Linda answered. "It depends whether Dib is barren or not."

"What does that mean?" I asked.

"It means infertile," she said impatiently. "Miss Watson explained it all to us last week in the biology lesson. Weren't you listening?"

"Yes," I muttered, feeling uneasy.

The more I thought about it, the more worried I got. After all, some of the things that had been discussed that Friday evening about intercourse, ejaculation and masturbation, I knew about anyway. I know it's not a very nice thing to admit, but yes, as young as I was, I had been fucked. I had felt Nick ejaculate all over my belly and I knew that masturbation gave you sexual pleasure. There were a few more things that I knew as well but I wasn't going to say anything. I couldn't could I? I'd get Nick into trouble.

"Pinky, you look pale," Linda said, concern spreading across her face. "Are you all right?"

Making an excuse, I said, "I'm fine. "It's just that I've got some homework to do tonight before I go to bed. I'll see you tomorrow."

By the time I got home that evening, I was feeling rather queasy and was ready for my bed.

"You look tired." Mum said, whilst we were clearing up after supper.

"Yes, you do look tired." Dad said. "If I were you, I'd have an early night."

As I lay in bed drifting off to sleep, I decided that tomorrow, I would see Nick on my own. I wanted answers to a few questions and it wasn't just to find out whether Dib was cooking chicken noodle soup for the evening meal on Saturday.

A few days later, I went to see Dib and when Nick returned home that evening after being in the antique shop all day, he threw wads of money down on the floor, near to where I was sitting and said brusquely, "Potty, count this up for me."

I sat for ages sorting out the money and it wasn't until after I had separated all the notes and told him exactly how much was there, that he knew how much profit he had made that day. He trusted me implicitly.

The point was did I trust him?

Dib knew that there was something wrong between Nick and me and whilst I was helping her wash the dishes, she shut the kitchen door and quietly said,

"If you and I fall out, it doesn't matter. We both know that after we've said what we have to say, it's all forgotten and everything is back to normal." There was silence for a few minutes and then she said, "Pol, promise me something."

"Yes," I replied, without really thinking about the implications. "I promise."

"He's been going around like a bear with a sore head, arguing with everyone," she said, making a fist and pointing her thumb towards the adjoining wall. "He's mad. You know what he's like."

"He's been all right this evening," I replied, not really knowing what to say.

"That's because you're here," Dib continued. I know it's difficult sometimes, with Nick being the way he is, but he takes it out on me and everyone else if things don't go the way he wants them to, or you fall out with him. Before the night is out, will you and Nick please resolve your differences?"

"I promise," I replied, not realising the obligations that she had placed on my shoulders.

"And another thing," Dib said, as she put the kettle on to make a cup of tea. "Don't go out of your way to avoid him, or stop coming to see us."

"I won't." I said, giving her a hug

During the evening, I was hoping to get the opportunity to speak to Nick whilst he was on his own but before I had a chance to say anything to him, he said, "You all right Pot?"

"Yes," I replied, looking him straight in the eye.

Nonchalantly, he said. "I told you there was no need

to worry, didn't I?"

"I got sent home from school Monday, with a bad tummy ache," I told him.

"Was it bad?" he asked, affectionately putting his hand on my shoulder.

"Apart from not being able to go swimming, it wasn't too bad." I replied.

Over the last few days, a lot of thoughts had been going round in my head. It seemed longer than four days since we had sat out the garden, having coffee.

"Potty," Nick had asked. "Have you come on yet?"

"No," I replied, thoughtfully. "I'm a few days late."

I continued drinking my coffee but Nick was rather uneasy. "Let me know when you come on," he said, getting up off the chair. "If anyone else is around, just stroke your right ear lobe like this."

I watched him, stroking his ear lobe as he went indoors and for the remainder of the afternoon, he wasn't in a good frame of mind. I tried to speak to him before I went home, but he was so abrupt and curt, that I had wondered what I had done wrong. It wasn't until I saw him coming out of the back gate the following day, and made a movement with my hand to my ear, that he began to relax.

"Can you have children?" I asked Nick, when I eventually saw him on my own...

"I'm not sure," he replied. "I've been with a lot of ladies in my time and I've never fathered a child yet."

We continued chatting for a few more minutes, until Dib came out to join us.

By the look on her face, you could tell that she was tired. She looked exhausted.

"Everything O.K?" she asked.

"Yes Dib, I answered. "Everything's O.K."

Nick and Dib's attitudes were different toward me

than that of my parents and their way of life was different too. What was acceptable in one household was frowned on in the other. It was little things like Mum and Dad having dinner midday and tea at night and Nick and Dib having lunch mid-day and dinner at night that confused me. Which is correct?

Sometimes, if Mum and I had been to the pictures and passed the fish and chip shop, she would treat us to some chips for supper.

"Do you fancy cod and chips?" Mum asked.

"Yes please." I answered, taking in the smell of freshly cooked fish.

Open wrapped in newspaper, with salt and vinegar sprinkled on, we would eat them as we slowly made our way home.

"That's no way for a young lady to behave," Nick said, when he saw me the following day. I stayed very quiet while he loudly voiced his opinion. "Only common people eat in the street."

You can imagine how I felt.

Most Saturday evenings, I would go to Nick and Dib's for an evening meal and unbeknown to my parents, would sometimes have a glass of wine. After a bite to eat, we would sit and watch television. It was the only night, apart from special occasions, that I was allowed to stay up until ten o'clock. Sitting watching the serial 'Jekyll and Hyde' I thought it was really scary. What made things worse was that Nick tormented me afterwards, pretending to be the character on the television.

"Will you walk me home Dib?" I asked, soon after the programme had finished. "I feel really scared."

"It's all right," Dib replied. "Nick will walk you down the road."

"Come on Potty," Nick said, putting on his cap as

he made his way out the front door.

I was a bit apprehensive, walking home with Nick that night in case he frightened me again but we hardly spoke a word to each other. As soon as I saw my dad with Freckie, our cairn terrier, standing by the front gate in Willoughby Lane, I said, "Thanks Nick, I'll be all right now."

Running as quickly as I could to where my Dad was standing and seeing how flushed and breathless I was, he said. "What's wrong? Are you all right?

"Yes Dad," I replied, gasping between breaths. "I'm sorry I'm late."

That night, alone in my bed, I couldn't sleep. My mind just wouldn't accept that the television programme was only make-believe.

Generally, I was a quiet and placid child, but there were occasions, especially when I wanted to voice my opinion, that the words came out all wrong and I would end up feeling really anxious. Sometimes, the family would laugh at me and it wasn't until later, after whatever word I had used incorrectly had been explained to me, that I realised why. Speaking on the subject of the Queen's coronation, I once said confidently. "When the queen was coronated."

It took no more than a look to realise I had made a blunder.

"If it was the Queen's coronation," I said. "She must have been coronated."

Raucous laughter could be heard in the room and the more I tried to explain, the more in a muddle I got. Feeling really upset this particular day, because nobody would listen or try to understand how I felt, I got really angry. Like Mount Etna in Sicily, I erupted and all hell broke loose. In a rage, I shouted, all the time gesticulating with my hands, until eventually, the tears came and I sobbed my heart out.

"Sandra, I'm sure that if I tied your hands behind your back, you wouldn't be able to talk." Mum said, getting impatient with me.

After my tears had subsided and things had calmed down, I was asked very nicely by my mother to tidy up my bedroom and polish the furniture and linoleum floor, until it shone.

"There's no excuse," Mum said, handing me a tin of lavender polish and a duster when I strongly objected. "Your bedroom is a mess."

Mum had her own way of dealing with me. She knew it was pointless locking me in my bedroom now that I was older.

"Bert," she said, exasperated. "Anybody would think I was murdering her, the way she's carrying on".

Dad just shrugged his shoulders and said. "Don't worry Cis. She'll get over it.

When Big Nan was alive, she would lock me in the walk-in pantry if I was naughty and started showing off.

"You little bugger. How did you get out of there?" she said, when my face appeared at the kitchen door, only a short time afterwards.

Showing her the metal spoon that I had bent, I grinned and said. "With this."

She couldn't help but laugh and it turned into a game after a very short time. Like the little rascal that I was, I would deliberately ask to be locked in and before escaping, would help myself to a jelly that had been prepared for tea or a piece of fruit cake that she had baked earlier. I'm sure she left the food on the bottom shelf purposely.

CHAPTER SEVENTEEN

I will tell you now what I didn't tell Linda that evening whilst we were sitting in the pub gardens having a quiet chat. If my memory serves me correct, the first time I went abroad with Nick and Dib was in 1958. I was growing up fast. Yes, too fast for my own good.

"What's this for?" I asked innocently when Nick handed me a wad of pound notes.

With my blue eyes open in amazement, I looked at Nick, awaiting an answer. "Quickly, put it in your knickers," he whispered.

Going into the ladies toilets without anybody noticing, I quickly entered an empty cubicle and once the door was securely bolted on the inside, I removed the notes from my coat pocket and without question, I did as I was asked. Bewildered I wasn't. In fact, you could say that I was quite excited about the whole episode. But what was going on? Why was Nick being so furtive?

"Are you all right in there Pol?" called Dib, who had come looking for me.

"Yes," I called out, straightening my clothes. "I'll be out in a minute."

Without saying another word, after washing my hands in one of the small basins, Dib and I eventually met up with Nick, who was busy organising everything before we boarded the ship to take us to Calais. I was feeling slightly uncomfortable by this time, as you can imagine. Thankfully, the elastic in my navy blue school knickers held firm around the tops of my legs. Otherwise, we would all be in trouble.

What can I say about my first trip to France? I knew we were going on a ferry across the English Channel but the size of the ferry was a lot bigger than I had imagined. What surprised me was the amount of people and cars that went on board.

"What do you think of her?" Nick asked, once we had made ourselves comfortable in the lounge.

"I can't get over how big the ferry is." I answered, completely in awe of everything that was going on around me.

"Dib," I said, turning to face her as Nick went into the bar to get us all a drink. "Why does everybody refer to a boat or ship as if it were female?"

"It's just one of those things." Dib replied, looking rather pale. "It's the same with cars."

We continued our conversation for a little while and when Nick returned with the drinks, Dib took two tablets from a little pill box that she had in her handbag.

"What's the matter?" I asked, concerned.

"I'm feeling rather queasy," Dib said quietly. No need for you to worry, I always get like this when we cross the Channel."

"You don't get sea sick do you Potty?" Nick asked.

"I don't know. I've never travelled by sea before," I replied, suddenly realising that the sea was getting quite rough.

"She'll be all right," Dib said assuredly. "Stop worrying about her."

Before the ferry set sail, a steward had explained over the public address system what procedures had to be taken in case of an emergency. Both Nick and Dib had stressed that on no account must I go out on deck on my own.

"Come on Potty," Nick said, after escorting Dib to the cabin. "Let's go and get something to eat. I'm starving. I don't know about you?"

Walking along, I felt rather sore. The wad of pound

notes that Nick had given me for safekeeping had slipped further down my knickers and was chafing my tummy.

"Nick," I whispered as we entered the restaurant.

He didn't hear me. With the noise of the engines and general chatter of the passengers, my voice was inaudible.

"Nick," I said again.

"What's the matter?" Nick asked. "You're not feeling sick are you?"

I must admit, with the movement of the ferry, items on the table seemed to be moving of their own accord. I was beginning to feel rather odd.

"No, I replied. "It's just that…"

Nick realised my dilemma when he saw me holding my hand across my tummy. Taking me out on deck, without anybody else hearing, he said. "As we are out of the three mile limit, you can let me have that money now."

A few minutes later, with the money safely tucked in Nick's Jacket pocket, I felt more comfortable. I was relieved to be free of the responsibility.

"Why did you ask me to look after it?" I asked, being nosey.

"Never you mind," he answered.

He could see by the look on my face that I wouldn't let up until I knew the answer.

"Because," he said, when we were out of earshot of other people. "You're only allowed to take a certain amount of cash out of the country."

"Oh," I said, none the wiser.

"Come on. Let's go and have breakfast. They should be ready for us now."

A few hours later, we were safely on terra firma and after having a good meal in the hotel where we were staying in Wissant, we enjoyed a leisurely walk along the sand dunes nearby. No longer was the sea rough as it had been earlier. Now, it was calm and peaceful.

"We should all sleep well tonight Pol"

"Yes," I replied, yawning. "I must admit, I am tired."

Dib, who was feeling much better now, suggested we make our way back to the hotel.

"We'll follow that path and go back a different way." Nick said, pointing his finger in the direction of some buildings.

As we walked back towards the hotel, the streetlights gave out a warm orange glow and the local people who saw us seemed ever so friendly. Some acknowledged us with a nod; others spoke to us in their native tongue.

For the first few days, I thoroughly enjoyed myself, meeting new people and exploring the local area. Then, everything changed. Nick changed. I was too naïve or too gullible to realise what lay in store for me. Dib had stayed behind at the hotel resting and I was being taken for a ride to Cap Gris-Nez, where the American swimmer, Florence Chadwick had set off to swim the English Channel.

"Nick," I asked. "What are those buildings on the beach?"

"They are called pillboxes," he answered. "Concrete bunkers that were erected during the war."

It was then that I was put through an ordeal that was to change my outlook on life and I lost the innocence of my youth. Being told to get in the back of Nick's blue van, which was fitted out with sorbo rubber and then having my pants pulled down, whilst kneeling on all fours, I knew that what I was participating in wasn't right. It was then that I felt him inside me and it hurt.

All I knew at that time was that I wanted to cry out in pain but instead, just looked out of the small window that was situated at the back of the van and concentrated on the WWII pillbox on the beach until he was satisfied and had ejaculated all over the base of my spine.

"It's time we made our way back," he said, after I had pulled my knickers up and he had adjusted himself.

Climbing into the front seat of the van, I didn't say a word. Instead, I reached over and took a barley sugar from the tin of sweets that Nick kept in the glove compartment. I wasn't traumatised as I should have been but realised that this was the kind of thing that was going to be expected of me. Was it my fault that this had happened? Well, was it?

There were a lot of people staying at the hotel and I was introduced to a gentleman, who I was told, flew with the famous squadron that was affectionately called 'The Dam Busters.'

"Hello," I said, not really sure what to say to him.

"Hello Sandra," he said, trying to put me at ease. "My daughter's name is Sandra and she is interested in ballet too."

Feeling very vulnerable, with the gentleman and Nick now engrossed in a conversation that I didn't really understand, Edward, the proprietor's youngest son came to my rescue and in perfect English said, "Would you like to go for a walk?"

"Don't go too far." Dib said, acknowledging that it was ok for me to go with him.

Making our way out of the hotel, leading directly onto the sand dunes, I felt as free as a bird. It was a beautiful day and there were people taking in the sunshine, either walking or sunbathing in the sand dunes. Edward was relaxing to be with and made me laugh with all his fascinating stories.

Believe it or not, Taffy, the proprietor of the hotel, Edward's father, was a Welshman and many years before, he had fallen in love with a local girl, Mademoiselle Lefsetz. In due course, they got married and bought up a family of three children whilst living in the area and eventually bought the hotel, which through hard work and determination, they turned into a thriving business. The children were all well educated and now that they were older, helped with the running of the hotel. Taffy and his wife were beginning to enjoy life, knowing that their eldest son, John, was going to take over the business and Madeleine, their daughter, who was an excellent cook, helped in the kitchen and did a lot of the administration.

"It won't be long before I come to England," Edward said. "I am going to join the British Army."

"Are you allowed to do that?" I asked, knowing that he was French.

"Yes," he answered. "Because my father is Welsh, I have a duel passport and when I am in England, I will come to see you."

I was smitten and didn't believe for one minute that he would keep his word but yes, a few years later, he contacted Nick and Dib with the news that he had in fact joined the British Army and was being stationed overseas. Much to my surprise; Dib had invited him to the house for a meal whilst I was there and I couldn't get over how handsome he looked in his uniform.

"When you come to France again," he said, "let me know and I will take you to see the Eiffel Tower."

"I would like that." I said. "Thank you."

As it turned out, many years later, I did go to Paris with my second husband, Norman, and yes, I did go up the Eiffel Tower.

"The world belongs to the brave." A German lady said to me in broken English, when I made it known that I was not going any further than the second level.

"I'll wait in the restaurant." I said, trying not to show my anxiety.

Hiding behind a camera lens, I took some photographs from the observatory platform whilst Norman made his way up the steps to the next level and then I joined the queue to get something to drink.

"Un café s'il vous plaît." I said, in my best French accent.

"Here you are," said the waitress in perfect English.

Sitting quietly on my own, taking in the atmosphere, whilst drinking my coffee, I realised that life was an illusion and things weren't always what they seemed.

CHAPTER EIGHTEEN

Sometimes I think it is a good thing that things change. It's called progress. What I didn't realize was that on a personal level, events would take over that would change my life and I would learn the hard way how to stand on my own two feet and make my own decisions.

"I've spoken to Bert in the corn chandlers," Dad said, as we were having tea one evening, not long after I had returned from holiday with Nick and Dib. "There's a vacancy going for someone to help him in the shop and I told him that next Saturday, when I go and get the pigeon corn, I would take you with me so he can have a chat with you."

Not fully realizing the situation, I just said casually, "Can't go next Saturday as I have made arrangements to go dancing with my friends in the afternoon."

"Never mind about dancing," Dad said. "I have told Bert that you will be leaving school soon and will be able to go and work for him."

"I don't want to work in the shop at Bruce Grove." I said crossly. "I want to be a nurse and work in Great Ormond Street."

I was so upset that I couldn't finish my tea and when the tears flowed, I flounced out of the room and shut myself in my room. I was fourteen years of age

Miss Smith, the headmistress at St Katherine's, the school that I attended, knew I wanted to be a nurse and a few weeks beforehand had kindly made arrangements with the matron at Prince of Wales hospital to speak to me and to answer any questions that I had.

"Just don't be late for the appointment that I have arranged for you." Miss Smith said.

"No Miss." I said. "I won't."

On the day of the appointment, after catching two buses to Tottenham Green, I arrived at the hospital with my mother, who had agreed to come with me and together, we were taken to a waiting room.

"Mum. What time is it?" I asked after a little while.

"It's not eleven o'clock yet." Mum said, looking at the clock on the wall. "We did arrive ten minutes early. Now stop fidgeting."

"Yes Mum." I said.

The next thing we heard was matron walking down the hall talking to someone.

"Thank you sister," I heard her say.

"Good morning," matron said when she saw us, extending her hand to greet us.

After introducing herself, we were shown into an office where lots of books aligned the walls.

"Thank you for coming," she said. "Please take a seat."

A large mahogany desk, inlaid with leather, was in the middle of the room where matron sat and the buttoned chairs that we sat on were old but so comfortable. I'm sure that if I were to have closed my eyes I would have gone to sleep with the smell of fresh flowers permeating the room.

"Would you like me to open a window?" she asked.

The conversation that we had was very informal and I found matron to be a very kind lady. She wasn't at all austere like I imagined.

"Do well at school," she advised me as we were preparing to leave. "See a bit of life first and if you still want to be a nurse, come back and see me when you're seventeen."

"Thank you." I said shaking her hand.

As I said, things change. A few years later, when I

was seventeen, I had received a reply from Great Ormond Street Hospital and was in the process of going for an interview when I found out I was pregnant. That put the kibosh on things and because I wanted to keep the baby, any thoughts of me being a qualified nurse went out the window.

"Where does time go?"

Fast forward another thirty years and the building which was once Prince of Wales Hospital in Tottenham Green is now living accommodation. Instead of a hospital, the wards and operating theatres were converted into apartments and renamed Deaconess Court.

"Unbelievable."

What happened when I was fourteen? Yes, I did leave school at the end of March, when we broke up for the Easter holidays, and I never went back.

"Mum." I asked indignantly. "Why can't I stay on at school 'til I'm sixteen like Jackie and Frances and take my English and Math's exams?"

"Now don't start," she said. "You know that your father was very ill with pneumonia!"

"What has that got to do with me having to leave school?" I asked indignantly.

"For the nine weeks that your father was ill he never got paid and we can't afford for you to stay on at school." Mum said, looking really worried.

To say that I was upset was an understatement. I was so annoyed that she wouldn't listen to what I had to say that my voice got louder and louder.

"I don't want to work in the corn chandlers." I shouted.

"Now that's enough," she said pointing her finger toward the door. "Now go and tidy the mess in your bedroom. I don't want to hear another word from you!"

Eventually, things calmed down and I had no option but to do what was expected of me. Before you knew it, I had left school and after a few weeks of working in the shop, I had learned how to use the cash register and helped the customers with their groceries. The delicatessen counter sold lots of different cold meats and cheeses and on one occasion, after I had washed my hands, I was shown how to cut cheese with a wire.

"Whatever you do, don't use the slicing machine." Bert said. "The blades are very sharp and I don't want you having any accidents."

I was beginning to enjoy myself and when the corn and maize was delivered, the big sacks were emptied into bins on the other side of the shop where Bert would make a point of talking to the customers, some of whom were pigeon fanciers, like my dad, about race meetings and the like.

Coming back from my lunch break one afternoon, Bert called me over wanting to have a chat with me about a delivery that had arrived. To be honest, by the tone of his voice, I thought I had done something wrong. He made me feel really uncomfortable.

"You know the delivery that we had this morning," he said.

"Yes," I replied, remembering that the delivery driver had emptied some corn and maize into the bins.

"Look," he said crossly, going over to the bins. Turning the corn over in his hand, he said. "Some of this corn has got holes in." Without drawing breath, he muttered, "I want you to sort through this batch and separate them."

When I heard what he had said, I thought he was joking.

"You want me to separate each piece of corn that has got a hole in it!" I exclaimed, taking on the enormity of the task.

"Yes," he said harshly.

After sorting through the corn for about half an hour, with the dust particles getting down the back of my throat, I'd had enough. 'Sod this for a game of soldiers,' I thought.

"Is that all you've done?" Bert shouted as he looked over my shoulder a little while later. "I want all that finished by the time you go for your break this afternoon."

What came over me, I don't know but I wasn't going to be spoken to in that manner. I appreciated that a bad batch of corn had been delivered but it wasn't my fault. I was so incensed at the way he spoke to me that it made me realize that I didn't want to work for him anymore and I told him so. As my eyes filled up with tears, he said. "You'd better get your coat then."

Without hesitating, I went through to the back of the shop, washed my hands and grabbed my windcheater that was hanging on the peg.

"Goodbye." I muttered, as I hurried out of the shop into the fresh air.

As I walked outside, making my way down Bruce Grove, I threw my head back, took in a gulp of fresh air and said out loud.

"Freedom, I don't have to go back there anymore."

It had been raining that morning but now that the sun was trying to come out, it was quite pleasant. I was in no hurry to get home and before getting to the High Road, I noticed that one of the shops in the main street had been refurbished. I couldn't understand the Chinese writing that was displayed above the shop front but glancing in the window, it was apparent that it was going to be a restaurant. Lots of tables and upholstered dining chairs had been strategically placed around the room and large silk embroidered pictures hung from the walls. I was fascinated, especially when I saw two young ladies wearing colourful Chinese cheongsam dresses, covering the tables with deep red table cloths and matching napkins.

"Can I help you? The owner said, as he came out of the shop doorway.

"What does that mean?" I said, trying to hide my embarrassment, pointing my finger to the sign.

"Inn of sixth happiness," he said in broken English.

"Thank you." I said, not knowing what else to say.

"You come eat in the restaurant when it's open. I will give you chop sticks."

"Thank you." I said again, glancing at the menu that he had given me.

As I continued walking down the street, I suddenly realized that I should have collected some paperwork from Bert before I left the shop. What do I do now? I was worried but I certainly wasn't going to go back for it. Apart from that, what was my Dad going to say when he came in from work and I told him I had walked out of the job. I was miles away and the next thing I knew, someone was calling out my name.

"Sandra. Are you all right?"

When I looked, it was Flo, a workmate of my Mum's, who was making her way to the bus stop. "Yes thank you." I answered politely, trying to stop my bottom lip from quivering.

"You don't look all right to me" she said, seeing the worried expression on my face. "Anyway, what are you doing down this part of the world?"

When I told her about the job and what had happened, she listened intently to what I had to say and then her face broke out into a broad grin.

"I don't blame you for walking out," she said.

"Sorting out the pigeon corn with holes in, I ask you. I'm sure your Dad will have something to say about that!"

By the end of the conversation, she made me laugh so much that tears were rolling down my cheeks.

"Stop making me laugh." I chortled. "I'll wet myself in a minute."

Flo was a rotund lady and having bought up seven children, there wasn't anything that you couldn't tell her. She had such mischievous eyes and when she laughed, her whole body shook and her face took on a rosy glow. You knew all about it though if you lied to her or was disrespectful. I'd heard her more than once raise her voice in anger when I'd been to her house over the years.

"I tell you what," she said, as we walked along the High Road. "Why don't you see if you can get a job in Woolworths? I know that they were taking on Saturday girls."

"That's a good idea," I replied as we mounted the 233 bus at the top of Northumberland Park. "I'll call in to see them tomorrow."

"Just mind how you go," she said.

When I got home, I left it to my mother to explain why I had walked out of the job and even though Dad wasn't very pleased at the time, after thinking about things, he said that when he called in the shop to see Bert on Saturday morning, he would have a chat with him and collect the rest of my belongings.

"What are you going to do now?" he asked inquisitively.

"I'm going to get a job in Woolworths." I said confidently.

"Don't be so sure," he said as he donned his cap, going outside to feed the birds. "You don't know if they've got any jobs available yet."

The following morning, even though I felt apprehensive, I was determined to find out about the job before my nerves got the better of me.

"Hope you get on all right." Mum said, as she was leaving for work. "Just don't forget to make sure that the door is locked when you go out."

"Yes Mum." I said, without really listening to what else she was saying.

Only a few hours later, I was introduced to the manager of the store in Tottenham and shown into an office to discuss working for them on a part time basis.

"Thank you Mr. Bellini." I said at the end of our conversation.

"Start here on Monday morning at 9 o'clock." he said abruptly.

"Before you go," his secretary said, "If you can just let us have your signature on these forms, we can sort everything out on Monday when you come in."

I was excited when I started walking home.

"Dad, I've got a job." I said as soon as he came in from work. I was elated.

"That's good," he said, taking his jacket off. "Your mother will be pleased. Where will you be working?"

"I will be working on the sweet counter at Woolworths." I told him proudly.

CHAPTER NINETEEN

I was settling into my new job and as I glanced over toward the main doors, who should I see walking up to the sweet counter with her shopping trolley was my Nan.

"Hello, can I help you?" I asked, knowing that I was being watched by a senior member of staff.

"Can I have a quarter of jelly babies please?" Nan said poker faced. "Just make sure that they are all boys."

Not sure if I had heard her correctly, I said, "Pardon."

By this time, another young girl, who was also being trained, came over and listened to the conversation.

"I want a quarter of jelly babies please." Nan repeated to the girl standing beside me. "Just make sure that they are all boys."

The poor girl, Liz, was confused. "Apart from being different flavours, I thought they all looked the same," she said

By this time, I could see the corner of my Nan's mouth twitch and knew she was kidding.

"You get more for your money if you have the boy ones."

I couldn't believe that when my colleague scooped up some jelly babies to put on to the weighing scales, we both actually looked to see if there was any difference in the shape.

"Thank you." Liz said, as she handed Nan her sweets.

By this time, with Nan's back towards us, pulling her shopping trolley in the direction of the exit sign, we couldn't contain ourselves.

"Who was that?" Liz asked questioningly.

"Shush! That was my Nan," I answered, grinning.

With that, we both burst out laughing and were sent on our break early to calm down. Nan certainly made her presence known that afternoon.

Sitting at home on a cold November evening, listening to the radio after having a healthy meal, it was announced that there was going to be a bus strike in North London the following day and commuters would have to make their own way to work. .

"What's that all about Dad?" I asked.

"A dispute in pay," Dad answered abruptly.

"Trouble is, they don't know when their well off." Mum said, almost as an afterthought.

"Does that mean I can have the day off tomorrow? I asked Dad exuberantly.

"No you can't." he replied crossly. "You'll walk to work like everyone else."

The following morning, I left for work early and quite enjoyed the walk into work. It was cold and windy but with a thick scarf wrapped round my neck and wearing a pair of hand knitted gloves that my Nan had made for me, I didn't feel the cold at all. To be honest, it gave me time to think. To all intents and purposes, I should be happy without a care in the world. At 15 years of age, I had a regular job working for Woolworths, was helping with the finances at home by giving my Mum thirty five shillings a week and had money in my purse to have my hair done at Duvall's Hair Salon in the High Road. What more could you ask for. Why then was I so unhappy? I was living a lie. It was all an illusion. A misconception!

Over the years, I had learnt to hide my feelings, put on a brave face and accept what life had to offer. After all, it wasn't all bad. There were some good times too!

"Come on Sandra. Chin up. Back straight and walk into a room as though you own it." I remembered our music teacher, Miss Whitehead, saying.

"Yes Miss." I would answer timidly.

"Where's that smile?"

The only way that I kept sane was through music and dance. With a few friends, on a Saturday afternoon, if we weren't roller skating at Alexandra Palace or Ally Pally as it is known, we would go to the Municipal building in Tottenham where they had a resident band. For the time we were there, everything else was forgotten. Listening to the music and dancing our socks off, we could actually feel the rhythm of the music through the soles of our feet. I remember on one occasion being allowed to go to a dance at the 'The Royal' in the High Road on a Saturday night.

"Just stay together and don't get into any trouble," Mum said as we were leaving.

The atmosphere in the dance hall was electric and it was during the 1960's that a lot of bands played there, including 'The Who' and a local pop group 'Dave Clarke Five'.

At home, Mum and Dad were kind people. They worked hard and gave me everything they could afford. Why then were they completely oblivious to the fact I had been sexually abused for years. I didn't realize it myself at the time but from the age of three, after Nick was demobbed from the Air Force, I was being maltreated. I didn't comprehend that what was happening to me wasn't acceptable behavior.

"How did it all start?" I was asked by a psychiatrist some years later.

"Apparently, I was to blame." I answered guiltily. My eyes were now focusing on a dirty mark that was on the patterned carpet beneath my feet. "It was my fault."

"Isn't it strange how the abuser can blame their misdeeds on an innocent child?"

I wasn't even old enough to go to school when things first started to happen. There I was fast asleep, lying on the big double bed with Dib's husband, after having Sunday lunch. Would you let a young child go to bed for the afternoon with a man she hardly knew? Were people that naïve? It appears that whilst asleep in the bed, when I turned over to make myself comfortable, my hand rested on his cock. Can you believe that? Instead of gently removing my hand, he got some kind of gratification from it and the seed was sown in his mind to pursue this game to its final conclusion.

In this day and age they call it grooming and yes, children are still being sexually abused and exploited all the time, despite parents and teachers being aware of the dangers. Often, the abuser is known to the family and the children are too frightened to speak out. Who would believe them anyway?

"She's got a vivid imagination," some would say.

"He's telling lies again," say others.

Yes, it does happen to little boys too. These children are confused and when they come to realize what is happening to them, what can they do? Unless someone takes time to listen to them or see the sadness in their eyes, what other option have they got but to withdraw into themselves? Some children become disruptive and naughty, others run away. Trouble is, if a child runs away from home and the police find out where they are, more often than not they get taken back to their parents with a flea in their ear and the sexual abuse starts all over again, only this time much worse. It's different if a child gets shouted at or walloped by their Dad. At least that is some kind of communication but to be sexually abused at a very young age is not only traumatic but can lead to psychological disorders.

"You have a personality disorder." I was told later in life by the psychiatrist.

"What does that mean?" I asked, completely bewildered.

Not getting a satisfactory answer from the psychiatrist, I was getting upset and confused. Changing her tactic, she said. "What school did you go to? Were you happy as a child?"

So many questions were asked of me and after having a glass of water and given a handkerchief to wipe the tears from my eyes; I composed myself and began to tell her what I thought she wanted to know.

"Settling back into the infant school, after being ill, I soon caught up with my lessons." I told her. "The teachers were very pleased with my progress and at the end of term; I was given a good report."

"Did you make friends at school?

"As much as I wanted to fit in with my school friends, they treated me differently. Nan, my maternal grandmother was always there to take me to school and fetch me home and I wasn't allowed to walk to school with the other children or mix socially with them."

Seeing my distress, Dr Skinner was very kind to me and said.

"That is enough for today. What I would like you to do next time you come to see me is to get yourself an exercise book and start writing things down as you remember them."

"Where do I start?" I asked, perplexed.

"Where else to start but at the beginning," she said smiling. "Writing things down is good therapy."

146

It was because of her kind words and me jotting down a few sentences in a notebook that I decided to write a few short stories relating to things that had happened to me. Surprisingly, my notebook was soon full with odd little facts and things that I had remembered over the years. Little notes that I had written were now becoming essays and like Topsy, a character in the novel Uncle Toms Cabin, the stories just grew and grew until the first few chapters of this book was written.

It didn't take too long to walk to Woolworth on that bitterly cold morning. Meeting a few of my work colleagues along the way, we ambled along, laughing and chatting as if we didn't have a care in the world. In the canteen, the management thanked us for getting to work on time despite the bus strike and we were all given a nice hot mug of tea and a biscuit before the shop opened.

CHAPTER TWENTY

I enjoyed working in Woolworth's, especially now that I was in the cash office collecting money from the tills and cashing up. Mum was pleased for me when I first got promotion and it meant that I could give her a few extra shillings housekeeping each week. Not only that, but the responsibility that came with the job gave me the confidence that I needed to use the telephone and be more assertive.

Using a Burroughs adding machine, I learnt to input the figures from each till and then pull down a handle so that the calculations could be printed off. There weren't any calculators like there are today. Half way through doing the cashing up, if the figures were illegible or didn't print at all because the ink had run out, then we had to enter the information all over again once Ella, the chief cashier, had put a new ribbon in the machine.

It was a responsible job being in charge of over twenty tills and with only two cashiers, the job was very time consuming. Sometimes we had to stay late if there was a discrepancy with the money but in the majority of cases it was just a miscalculation and the mistake was soon rectified. It was a different scenario when a member of staff decided to help themselves to money that didn't belong to them. On this occasion, the necessary action was taken and the employee lost their job.

I had only been working in the office a few months and because we were short of staff and the fact that we were so busy, instead of walking to the canteen, I was taking my lunch break in the back office when all hell broke loose.

"What's going on?" I asked, rushing through to find out what the commotion was all about.

"The security guards are here to collect the money," my colleague said, looking worried. "The trouble is, the safe is locked and Ella has gone to the Post Office to get some stamps and the store manager is not in the building."

You can imagine the atmosphere in the small office. Everyone was getting tense and the guards, in all their attire and safety helmets, were about to leave when the duty manager came into the office.

"You don't know the combination of the safe, do you?" he said, looking at us helplessly.

"No," we both said in unison.

"Do you want me to have a go?" I said smugly.

"How are you going to open the safe!" he said, exasperatedly.

"I have seen how they do it in films"

Without further ado, I put my ear on the cold steel surface of the safe and turned the dial slowly until I heard a distinctive click. Taking a pause, I slowly turned the dial the other way and again heard a distinctive click. After only a few minutes, much to the disbelief of everyone in the office, the door of the safe opened. I was dumbfounded. I couldn't believe it myself.

"How did you manage to do that?"

"You should get yourself a job as a safecracker."

I just put it down to sheer luck. I was and still am interested in the criminal fraternity and not only enjoyed watching gangster films, I also read a lot of true crime stories as well. Perhaps instead of wanting to be a nurse, I should have studied criminology and worked in a laboratory studying forensics. Who knows?

"I will lock the safe up now," the duty manager said after the security guards had left. For a brief moment, you could see trepidation in his eyes and looking directly at me and then at my colleague, he said quietly. "It's best that we don't say any more about what happened this afternoon otherwise we will all be in trouble."

Nodding in agreement, we acknowledged what he said and went about our business as normal as if nothing untoward had happened.

At sixteen years of age, with the right attitude and a National Insurance card, you could get a job anywhere and if you were prepared to travel, there were so many opportunities that were available to you. Jackie, my school friend, travelled to the City every day working for a filter paper company and Rosemary, another school friend, was now a full time student at Tottenham Technical College. Other friends had moved out of the area to pursue their careers in different parts of the country and here I was with itchy feet, disillusioned with life, impatient and wanting to start afresh somewhere new. Things had to change and fast. Otherwise, who knows what I was capable of!

"Have you made up your mind what you are going to do?" Auntie Rose asked me on one of her rare visits to see the family.

"I am just biding my time for when I'm seventeen and can start my training."

"I know that you were interested in taking up nursing as a career but I'm surprised that you don't go in the army," she said. "What about the Queen Alexandra's Nursing Corps? That sounds like a good job and you'll see a bit of life too."

"I have already received correspondence from Great Ormond Street" I told her and was confident that after my birthday in April, it was just a formality that I would start my training.

"Ever since you were a little girl, you've always wanted to be a nurse," she said. "If I were you, I'd go out and enjoy myself first and see a bit of life."

"That's what the matron at Prince of Wales Hospital said!" I exclaimed.

"Yes, and I agree with her," she said. "You're only young once, so don't be too hasty."

Auntie Rose was my mum's cousin and because of circumstances, Nan took her in when she was a little girl and Auntie Eileen, Mum and Auntie Rose were bought up like sisters. Rosie, as mum called her was a short rotund lady and what she lacked in height, she made up for in other ways. She had a great sense of humour and always made us laugh but woe betide you if you made her cross. I respected what Auntie Rose had to say and when she returned home to Cogenhoe, in Northampton with her daughter Stephanie, I was sorry to see them go.

"Sandra, what's this I hear about you leaving us?" one of my work colleagues asked a few months later, as I was getting ready to leave the premises.

"Yes, I said quietly. I have got a job in the office at Gibson's along the High Road."

"The turf accountants!" she exclaimed, looking surprised. "Aren't you too young to be working for a bookie?"

"I'll be working in the offices dealing with football coupons." I said. "I won't be working in the betting shops."

"Good luck," she said. "Don't forget to keep in touch. We are going to miss you."

The reason why I left Woolworths was because it was getting complicated. I enjoyed the job and met some interesting people but I was beginning to feel as though my every move was being watched.

"Is it my imagination?" I had asked Maggie, when we had a lunch break together. "I can feel Bellini's eyes following us. He is making me feel really uncomfortable."

"Oh my dear," she said brusquely. "Don't worry about him."

"I can tell you a few things about Bellini," said Maggie's friend, as she came to join us at the dining table. "He is like that with all the young girls. He is only keeping an eye on you. My advise to you is keep your head down, get on with your work and don't give him just cause to reprimand you, otherwise you will be in trouble."

It wasn't just because the manager was continuously staring at us or making snide remarks but Nick had started coming into the shop to talk to me, which I found distressing. On one occasion, he seemed to appear from nowhere whilst I was on the shop floor collecting the money from the tills.

"Potty," he shouted over the whirring of the freezers. "Come round after work. I want to talk to you."

Whilst carrying the money bags on my shoulder, he followed me round the store and I was beginning to feel vulnerable. Where was the duty manager when I needed him?

"I can't come round this evening." I said, raising my voice.

Looking rejected and disheveled, he said. "Dib's left me and I don't know how to cook the chicken."

I didn't know what to believe. Had Dib really left him after all these years? If she had left him, surely the last thing on his mind would be how to cook a chicken!

"I'll call in on the way home," I said, not knowing what else to say. "I have been invited out this evening so I won't stay long."

It was a relief when I saw him walk away but for the remainder of the afternoon, I was feeling anxious.

With the wind blowing in my face that afternoon, as I walked along the High Road after leaving work, I had time to think. My mind was working overtime and I was worried. I didn't want to be in the situation that I was in now. Turning into Park Lane and going past the Post Office, I stopped and spoke to a neighbor who was posting a letter.

"Are you on your way home?" he asked inquisitively.

"Not yet." I answered. "I am going to call in to see Nick first."

"You mind how you go," he said. "I saw him earlier and he's like a bull with a sore head. Don't know how his wife puts up with him the way he shouts and hollers."

Before going home, I felt obliged to call in and see Nick. I had given my word but knowing that Dib wasn't home made me wonder whether it was a ruse for Nick to get me alone in the house. As it turned out, my fears were unfounded. Nick was in a terrible state.

"I'll make you a cup of coffee." I said, not knowing what else to say

Having been invited for tea with John's family in Clarendon Road that evening, I hurriedly made him a coffee, which he washed down with another glass of whisky whilst I started to prepare the chicken.

"Have you any idea where Dib has gone?" I asked, as I watched him flick through Dib's address book.

"She may have gone to her sister's," he said, looking bewildered. "I don't know where else she would have gone."

After putting the chicken in the oven to cook, I decided to phone Aunt Emma, Dibs sister, hoping that Dib would be there.

"What's Aunt Emma's number?" I called out.

"It's in the book." I heard him say.

Fortunately, the telephone number was easy to find and after a few minutes I spoke to Dib.

"Don't worry," she said. "I'll be home in a few days. It's just that things were getting on top of me and I needed a break. It will do the old bastard good to be without me for a little while."

Confident in the knowledge that Dib would be home for the weekend, I hurriedly left the house before anything unpleasant happened. Without a backward glance or even saying goodbye, I made my way home, looking forward to the evening ahead.

Printed in June 2023
by Rotomail Italia S.p.A., Vignate (MI) - Italy